The SACRED ART of HUNTING

The SACRED ART *of* HUNTING

MYTHS, LEGENDS *and the* MODERN MYTHOS

BY JAMES A. SWAN, PH.D.

Willow Creek
PRESS

MINOCQUA, WISCONSIN

Published in 1999 by Willow Creek Press
P.O. Box 147, Minocqua, Wisconsin 54548

Permissions for Quotation from Published Works:
    University of Arizona Press
    William Morrow & Co.
    World Federation of KSI Muslim Communities
    Ted Nugent United Sportsmen of America
    General Norman Schwarzkopf

Cover Illustration and chapter head illustrations by Arlene Connolly. For more information about Arlene's "Petroglyph Preservations" please write to:
    Arleme Connolly
    P.O. Box 2909
    State Line, NV 89449

For information on other Willow Creek Titles, call 1-800-850-9453

Designed by Deb Claus

Library of Congress Cataloging-in-Publication Data

Swan, James A.
    The sacred art of hunting : myths, legends, and the modern mythos / by James A. Swan.
        p.   cm.
    ISBN 1-57223-188-2
    1. Hunting.   I. Title
    SK33.S92 1999
    799--dc21
                                99-38313
                                CIP

Printed in England

All hunters should be nature lovers.

Theodore Roosevelt

Other Books by James A. Swan:

Environmental Education (with Wm. B. Stapp)
Sacred Places
The Power of Place
Nature As Teacher and Healer
Bound to the Earth (with Roberta Swan)
In Defense of Hunting
Dialogues With the Living Earth

Acknowledgments

So many people aided this book's realization that I cannot list them all, but Chuck and Tom Petrie, Heather McElwain, John Jackson III, Dr. Yves Lecocq, Stephen Hewett, Michael Faw, Patrick Plante, Chuck Stapel, Jim Zumbo, Raymond Stroup, Lt. Col. Dennis Foster and Arlene Connally deserve a special note of appreciation.

TABLE OF CONTENTS

Hunters, an Endangered Species?

Throughout more than 99 percent of human history, hunting has been an unchallenged tap root of life, as well as a cornerstone of culture. Often, the success of hunters has meant the difference between feast or famine, and their exploits and service to the community have been celebrated in song and story, setting standards as positive role models. In fact, throughout nearly all of human history, hunters have been unchallenged cultural heroes.

In recent times, subsistence hunting has ceased to be a necessity of survival for most people. Sport hunting has become the norm. Each year, more than 15 million North Americans, 12 million Europeans, and many more millions elsewhere hunt for recreation, as well as for tasty wild food. The widespread popularity of sport hunting is relatively new in human history. It must be pointed out, however, that nonsubsistence hunting has been enjoyed in Europe, Asia and Africa for thousands of years, but primarily by a privileged few.

The reasons for the modern hunter going afield may differ from those of his ancestors. His beliefs, customs and culture are different, as is his access to many technological advances and gadgetry. But is the emotional experience of hunting much different for the modern hunter than it was for his Paleolithic ancestors? Probably not. Every modern hunter who sets foot on the trail of game has a thousand ancestors looking over his shoulder who have felt the same deep sentiments stir when looking down the sights of a gun or over an arrow at a majestic deer.

However, a most important difference for modern hunters is that they face determined social opposition. There is no evidence of any significant antihunting sentiment anywhere until the mid-20th century, even among cultures with large numbers of vegetarians. Today, however, all around the world modern hunters are subject to considerable scrutiny, criticism and even attack — socially, politically, and legally. The tide of antihunting sentiment has closed hunting seasons for certain species and regions, increased restrictions on methods of hunting, reduced acreage of huntable lands, decreased access to hunting lands, organized harassment in the field, harried hunters in their communities, leveled challenges in court rooms and won victories at the ballot box. Remarkably, all of this has taken place even though there are no valid ecological arguments against legal hunting guided by modern wildlife management sciences.

As they have come under attack, many ethical hunters have retreated from the public eye, becoming as secretive as the game they pursue. This makes it all the more likely that the hunters who end up in the evening news are the bad eggs. "The irony of the Information Age is that it has given new respectability to uninformed opinion," veteran newscaster John Lawton told the American Association of Broadcast Journalists in 1995. A question that deserves serious sociological study is why we have allowed the media to declare open season on heroes, while elevating the status of bold criminals to noteworthy news.

There appear to be several reasons for the recent shift in cultural attitudes about hunting:

1. About 5 percent of the American public hunts. In many foreign countries this percentage is even lower. Hunting, by nature, is a quiet sport, imbued with mystery, which takes place away from public view. The percentage of the public who hunts has grown smaller, and many people have lost first-hand familiarity with hunters. Consequently, hunting for many non hunters is foreign and fraught with suspicion.

2. The majority of the population has crowded into urban areas where increasingly

few people have any firsthand experience with nature, let alone with getting their hands bloody or dirty harvesting food to eat. Coupled with rising crime rates and biased media reporting that often paint hunting and firearms in a consistently negative image, this shift of population has made the hunter a convenient scapegoat for the projection of emotions tied to many of today's social problems, which have little to do with hunting.

3. Because of a focus on sensationalism, hunters suffer from a negative image created largely by the popular media, regardless of the improved safety of modern hunting — which is now much safer than many popular sports like tennis, swimming, touch football, and bicycle riding — and the increased sophistication of hunters, thanks to mandatory hunter education classes. It is a sad fact that poaching and hunting accidents get more attention in the general press than the considerable amount of good conservation work supported by the hunting community.

4. People have traditionally learned to hunt from family members. Today, with the breakdown of the nuclear family, 40 percent of all children will grow up in a single-parent family during their childhood, resulting in fewer role models and teachers to pass along the hunting heritage, especially in a more urban population.

5. Founded by Aldo Leopold, the science of wildlife management has made many advances since its birth some 60 years ago. There is no biological reason to oppose hunting guided by modern wildlife sciences. In fact, thanks to the cooperation of hunters and wildlife managers, most hunted species are more abundant today than a century ago.

Nonetheless, wildlife management education at many universities is endangered. Old schools of pragmatic natural resource management are being phased out, replaced by curriculums with a strong scientific and technological focus, as if machines were now the most important organisms in the ecosystem. Precious few college classes address hunting or fishing as human recreational pursuits. This trend places the future of hunting in further jeopardy as an increasingly small number of people who regulate hunting have any firsthand experience pursuing wily bucks in deep thickets, let alone scientific understanding of what runs through a hunter's mind.

6. Psychologists have not spent much time studying the motivations for hunting. The activity has been one of those things that people do, and no one has questioned it until very recently. In addition, the experiences of hunting occur far removed from the laboratory in environments that cannot be controlled. And, the experiences are often so profound that it is difficult to find words to adequately describe them. The lack of documentation makes it more difficult to defend hunting against false accusations, even when the accusers admit their charges are unfounded.

7. To be sure, there are some unethical "slob" hunters and hunting guides, but they are a tiny minority, thanks not only to laws and law enforcement, but also to the community of hunters who refuse to tolerate unethical hunting. In many areas, illegal poachers, though few in number, now kill more deer than legal hunters. Often, when we hear about hunting causing extinctions in various parts of the world, no one mentions that it is illegal hunting that is the problem.

The modern hunter is often stigmatized, scapegoated and stereotyped as a sadistic, mentally disturbed, unlawful, criminally inclined and dangerous person by a well-financed and dedicated animal rights antihunting movement, regardless of what science has to say about the safety and sanity of hunting. Just as bright sunlight cuts through heavy fog, the cutting blade of truth best dispels clouds of misinformation and false innuendo.

Setting the Record Straight

In his 1969 Pulitzer prize-winning book, *So Human An Animal*, the noted microbiologist Rene DuBos eloquently speaks of the significance of hunting to modern man:

> *Even though he lived by hunting, primitive man worshiped animals. In modern man also, the desire to hunt is paradoxically compatible with love of wild life. Hunting is a highly satisfying occupation for many persons because it calls into play a multiplicity of physical and mental attributes that appear to be woven into the human fabric . . . Certain aspects of a hunter's life are probably more in keeping with man's basic temperament and biological nature than urban life as presently practiced.*[1]

DuBos is an eminent humanist, but he was a microbiologist by training. He speaks from his heart, not as a behavioral research professional. Can social science also support his point of view?

Despite vitriolic accusations by some anti-hunters, there is no substantial psychological research or writing to conclude that hunting in general is in any way associated with mental disease. What evidence there is supports just

BULL ELK SHEDS ANTLERS

the opposite position. Many of the best-respected behavioral scientists of our times, including Sigmund Freud, William James, Carl Jung, Erich Fromm, Marie-Louise von Franz and Karl Menninger, have agreed that hunting is a natural, healthy part of human nature, an instinct programmed into the master computer of our species for survival purposes.

Dr. Erich Fromm, one of the most widely respected behavioral scientists of the 20th century, summed up these opinions in his acclaimed study of the causes and prevention of violence, *The Anatomy of Human Destruct-iveness*, which the eminent anthropologist Ashley Montague heralds as, "the best book I have ever read on the subject." Fromm finds:

In the act of hunting, a man becomes, how-ever briefly, part of nature again . . . (whether we are talking about the primitive hunter or the modern passionate hunter). The psychology of hunting, including that of the contemporary hunter, calls for extensive study, [but] . . . there is a considerable body of information about still existing primitive hunters and food gatherers to demonstrate that hunting is not conducive to destructiveness and cruelty . . . . Sadism (which has been alleged to be characteristic of modern hunters by some antihunting activists) is much more frequently to be found among frustrated individuals and social classes who feel powerless and have little pleasure in life.[2]

In his award-winning book, *The Tangled Wing*, based on his seven-year study of the bio-logical origins of human behavior, Dr. Melvin Konner, Emory University professor of psychi-atry and anthropology, agrees: "A few years ago it was a common belief that the evolution of human hunting had important implications for the nature of human aggression. This is not likely . . . there is little or no evidence, physio-logical or behavioral, to suggest that predatory aggression has much in common with intraspecies aggression."[3]

There has never been a serious scientific inquiry into the motivations of hunters in gen-eral that has found hunting to be anything other than healthy human behavior. And, in one of the rare studies of the relationship between gun ownership and crime among juveniles, high-school-aged boys who legally owned guns were found to have lower rates of delinquency and drug abuse than those who owned no guns.[4] Many social scientists, such as Colin Turnbull, even go so far as to note that many hunting peoples are especially peaceful and happy.

Ask passionate hunters why they hunt. Invariably, they will admit that in the final analysis hunting for them is much more than a recreational pursuit. Given time and trust, ulti-mately, they will say that for them hunting comes closer to being a religion.

What is religious about hunting is that it leads us to remember and accept the violent nature of our condition, that every animal that eats will in turn one day be eaten. The hunt keeps us honest.

DUDLEY YOUNG[5]

If we lose the animals, we lose our souls.

DAVE WATSON, *Last Stand In The Rockies*

Hunting the Spirit of the Hunt

Spending just half an hour a week alone in a natural setting can have positive therapeutic value for the modern anxiety-prone urbanite. Setting aside schedules, meetings, newspapers, television, and telephones, and allowing the mind to unwind and seek out its roots, is at the core of healing. And this is just the beginning. Research has shown that viewing natural scenery that has great beauty, such as majestic snow-capped mountains or spectacular bodies of water, is a common trigger of religious feelings. Nature, it seems, wants to help us discover our spiritual side as part of the wondrous force of ecological balance. This is of great importance to the survival of our species, as well as all life. We care most for what we love.

One of the greatest joys of nature is when we witness some of its deepest secrets. Wildlife photographer Gerry LaMarre must be blessed with the elk spirit and some extraordinary good luck. One day, while watching a herd of tule elk, he had his camera tracking two bulls, expecting one to engage the other in jousting. What he got was the shot of a lifetime: a bull elk shedding its antlers (see photo on page 11). LaMarre explains: "At that moment, the front bull stopped and in one swift twisting motion, he had disappeared from my camera's field of view. The front bull's sudden body motion of two 360-degree twists produced sufficient force for both antlers to snap off the crown simultaneously, without striking the adjacent bull."

Whatever nature does to us, hunting amplifies the experience. As the hunter's moon rides across the fall skies, in the quiet hours of first dawn, crouched in a duck blind as streams of waterfowl swarm toward the decoys, or sitting motionless on a deer stand in the snow-blanketed woods as an eight-point buck approaches, nature's magic stirs upwellings in the waters of the psyche. As hunting season approaches, sleep wanes. Senses become more alive. Sounds, odors and moods intensify. Signs of nature take on special meaning. The world becomes more vivid and time loses importance as being takes control of consciousness. Lethal weapons are taken up with loving hands. The blood of majestic creatures is spilled. Passions soar. Danger always lurks nearby. Hunting is filled with emotions, many of which are unique to the hunter and associated with the deepest roots of our being.

Hunting evokes strong feelings, but how can it be *religious?* Let's begin by getting our terms straight. In his insightful study of the spiritual roots of sport, The Sacred Origin and Nature of Sports and Culture, Prince Ghazi bin Muhammad, Ph.D. offers the following definition of terms:

> . . . *religion — from the Latin "religio," means to "bind" — is a revealed set of moral teachings and (usually) sacred laws through which man learns about God, his own true theomorphic nature, his ultimate end, either in Heaven or hell, and how to influence this end through belief, prayer, shunning evil deeds, and performing good ones.*
>
> *Mysticism is, on the other hand . . . something holy and numinous, a sacred wisdom.*[6]

Contacting the base of life, one feels the awesome presence of organic spirituality, what religious scholar Rudolph Otto called "numinous" — the vital, emotional presence of the Divine. Hunting is a very numinous experience because hunters kill. Killing something truly beautiful and beloved forces hunters to cultivate humility that is an essential building block for the art of loving. A billion words have been spoken about love, and none have truly hit the mark. Love is ultimately beyond words. Hunting is filled with profound emotions and passions that many would equate with mystical experiences. Managing those emotions and the passions they stir is what makes hunting religious.

Managing the Spirit of the Hunt

Regardless of whether the hunter is a bushman with a spear, a freckled-faced teenager with a .22 rifle and a beagle chasing a rabbit, or a baron swinging a $10,000 Beretta over-and-under after a fleeing grouse, and despite his beliefs — animistic shaman, Christian, Muslim or Buddhist — the hunter is a rider on a powerful dark horse, inspired by the spirit of the wild. A hunter is a passionate killer who shoots from the heart, embracing the dark to see the light. As psychologist Marie-Louise von Franz has written:

> Living means murdering from morning to evening; we eat plants and animals . . . plants suffer . . . so vegetarians cannot have the illusion that they do not share in the wheel of destruction. We are murderers and cannot live without murdering. The whole of nature is based on murder . . . The realization of the destruction and the wish to live are closely connected.[7]

When such powerful energies are unleashed, discipline, restraint and care are necessary to avoid excess. Success in mastering the potent energies of the hunt is one more reason why most cultures have seen hunters as heroes, for a hero, by definition, acts as a role model to set the standards of behavior for his culture.

Modern wildlife science has given us laws, grounded in research, that establish legal limits of hunter behavior to maintain ecological balance. Hunter heroes abide by the laws, but

there is much more to being an ethical hunter than being just law-abiding. Hunters who hunt from the heart are guided by higher laws.

Symbolism, ethical codes, philosophy, mythology, prayer, faith, doing good deeds, avoiding sins, fasting, ceremonies and rituals are just a few of the tools that hunters call upon to ensure that the true spirit of the hunt prevails. Most have a religious context. Listing all the practices used by traditional and modern hunters is well beyond the scope of this book and runs the risk of getting lost in the thickets of cultural anthropology.

To find game, a hunter learns to discern patterns of nature. To understand the spirit of the hunt one must look for overarching themes in the complex wilderness of hunting customs and beliefs. One model for understanding the spirit of the hunt is to see hunting as an expression of the archetypal journey of the hero, as mapped out by that wise guide to the deep forests of the soul, mythologist Joseph Campbell.

Going hunting requires following the steps of the hero's quest: a retreat from conventional society, surrendering to a sense of intuitive calling that leads one into mysterious realms, undertaking certain tasks which may involve danger. Deep emotions — excitement, awe, sadness — are faced, powers are taken on, strange teachers appear, personal transformation unfolds, heroic deeds are performed, and finally the hero returns as the "changed one" to serve the needs of the community and infuse fresh spirit into the lives of all.[8]

In the following pages we will trace the hunter's journey, and consider the value-laden issues flushed out at each step of the way, as well as examine some of the acts and customs that unite the mundane and transcendental elements of hunting. The language of the spirit of the hunt is complex. It requires images and metaphor to most closely approximate its essence. On this journey we must call on more of our senses (which Chinese sages insist number 100), and listen to the quiet voices on the wind and the passion in our hearts to dialogue with the spirit of the hunt.

Hunting submerges man deliberately in that formidable mystery and therefore contains something of a religious rite and emotion in which homage is paid to what is divine, transcendent, in the laws of nature.
Jose Ortega y Gasset[9]

. . . there are no words that can tell the hidden spirit of the wilderness, that can reveal its mystery, its melancholy, and its charm.
Theodore Roosevelt, *African Game Trails*[10]

The Hunting Instinct

*Neither in body nor in mind do we inhabit the world of those hunting
races of the Paleolithic millennia, to whose lives and life ways we
nevertheless owe the very forms of our bodies and structures of our minds.
Memories of their animal envoys still must sleep, somehow, within us;
for they wake a little and stir when we venture into wilderness.*

JOSEPH CAMPBELL[1]

The sun is quickly slipping below the snow-capped peaks to the west. As darkness floods in, wiping away our shadows, we begin back down the trail towards camp, the lingering memories of a day afield keeping our spirits high. It is fall. Summer is dying and winter's spirit penetrates the air with fragments of prophesy: golden, yellow, brown and red leaves floating to the ground; strings of ducks and geese passing southward through the skies; and, especially, cold blasts of frigid air that come rushing down from the North Pole, providing raw materials for Jack Frost's paint brush.

Autumn is the time to reap summer's bounty in anticipation of winter's shortage. We harvest grain and meat with metal — blades and bullets. This must be why the ancient Chinese sages divined that the element of fall is metal. Fall is a time of excitement, quickening, and of death. As the hunter's moon passes overhead, some of the most profound of all instinctual energies well up as nature plays us like musical instruments according to her moods. Of all the full moons of the year, none has as much meaning as the hunter's moon.

The call of the hunt is a mysterious force that draws people out into often the worst of weather, sacrificing sleep, taking risks, and often for little or no material success. Like sexual desire, cravings for food, water and shelter, and the desire to join with others of our species for companionship, the hunting instinct is a strong river of the psyche filled with mystery that lights fires in the souls of many people. That the hunter's moon, which pulls so much upon the water element around us and in us, makes that fire of soul burn brighter is one of those mysteries of nature that seems best understood by wily old stags and migrating geese.

Our reverie slips away quickly as a dark cloud suddenly snakes around a mountain like a flash flood. Suddenly the air is filled with swirling flakes of snow. A blast of the cool north wind slaps our faces. This is "the first breath of winter" the old timers talk about, an early cold storm that appears as the hunter's moon passes across the autumn skies. In earlier times or other cultures, the same weather might also be called "The Bear's Breath," a warning sent by the Great Bear spirit, keeper of the North Pole, that his season is coming.

The storm worsens. We cannot risk the remaining trek to camp. We must find shelter quickly. Up ahead, in a break between flurries, the yawning mouth of an old cave becomes visible. We dive into the inky black hole just as visibility is swallowed by a white cloud.

The wind outside howls like a hungry wolf pack. Gathering some dry wood together, we strike a match and invoke the powers of brother fire, recreating one of the greatest discoveries in human history. As the flames leap skyward, the walls of our shelter suddenly come to life. Behold! We are not the first. Pictographs and petroglyphs of animals — geese, cranes, stag, bear and bison — pursued by humans carrying spears and bows and arrows look down at us from every direction. We are squatters in the midst of an ancient art gallery. A hunter's cave.

Caves are an incubation chamber, a womb of mystery. Hunter's caves are special niches of natural magic, vessels that conserve the heritage of man's oldest occupation. Spirals, rams, elk, deer, hoof prints, clouds, sun, men with deer antlers on their heads and snakes glare down at us. Franz Boas once remarked, "There can be no doubt that in the main, the mental characteristics of man are the same all over the world."[2] The truth of his words is felt in a hunter's cave as much as in any other art gallery in the world. Art is a universal language. If a native hunter suddenly burst into this cave, spoken words might not be understood, but if we drew simple pictures of deer, bows and arrows, clouds, water and fire, to

explain our presence, communication would be immediate. He would quickly recognize that we shared the same god.

The storm shows no signs of letting up. Our technological oracle, the cellular phone, tells us that the storm will pass by morning. Our position has been pinpointed by a satellite orbiting in outer space that reports an approaching weather front is bringing clear skies with a high-pressure area (information our ancestors may have received from voices in the silence that we have long forgotten or dismissed as superstition). With the phone, we reassure the people in camp that all is well, and settle in. A required course in nature's university is humility.

This storm is a blessing in disguise. Freed from schedules and worries about the stock market and deadlines, we gaze at the simple images etched in stone and the gears of perception shift into overdrive. In this womb of the living being that the Pueblo Indians refer to as the "second mother," the earth, our minds soon shift into metaphoric gear, which is dominated by creativity and curiosity. The spirit moves us to explore. With burning branch in hand we probe the cave.

The ancient Greeks spoke of the personality or spirit of each place, its "genus loci." The landscapes we visit move us, especially when the spirit of a place is strong. Artifacts, petroglyphs, memories hovering in the air like invisible hawks — land has a memory that minds us. Hunter's caves are home to one very powerful spirit. In the silence, it speaks to us, perhaps even through us.

Behind a rock lies an empty metal rifle shell casing from a Sharp's rifle, evidence of hunters using this cave a century before. Scraping around in the dust, we unearth an obsidian arrowhead that speaks of Indians that sought shelter here a century or two ago. Digging deeper, we come upon a flint spear point that might have once been used to bring down a huge hairy mammoth or saber tooth cat, such as roamed these hills as the last glaciers slipped away some 10,000 years ago.

Fragments of bone recall ancient kills and feasts that surely spawned tales tall and true; probably the basis for some of the art on the walls. Rock art galleries in hunter's caves were the first trophy rooms. Four-fifths of the rock art in caves in France and Spain depicts edible animals.

Excavations in Africa report finding bone spearheads at least 80,000 years old. In Germany, six seven-foot-long spears found beside piles of animal bones have been dated at 400,000 years old. Some speculate that man has been a hunter for 3 million years. Others assert that hunting is the master pattern of our species. Anything that has been with us so long must be ingrained in our bones, blood and brain. The urge to hunt lives in all of us to varying degrees.

Hunting has its mundane side — mastering marksmanship, caring for one's weapons, wearing the proper clothing, following laws, buying licenses, butchering and caring for the game. Each year new clothing styles and gadgets call seductively to those afflicted with hunting fever. Modern technologies are better than those of our ancestors, but the energies of the hunt in the modern, passionate hunter arise from the same pool of primal spirit that stirred the brain, blood and bones of our Paleolithic ancestors. Just how we are like our ancestors becomes a Zen koan to ponder this long night.

Mining the Soul
Some rock art may simply be ancient bulletin boards, calendars, records and autographs — maybe even graffiti. However, other handiworks of our ancestors seem to shoot lightning bolts of insight, a power some Indian tribes assert comes to us through the eyes of the giant thunderbird who lives in the western sky. If he visits us in a dream tonight, a modern psychologist will say it is a fragment of our unconscious. A native shaman would assert the giant black bird is a spirit. Either way, the thunderbird is an ally who frequents hunters' caves.

Around the world, the story lines of great tales, pictorial renditions of sagas and declarations of territoriality are immortalized in rock art at special sacred places. In other places, the figures are warnings or prophecies. Clearly, some cave art honors memorable kills, the first trophy rooms. Pictographs and petroglyphs may also venerate great hunters, warriors and shamans, not only honoring their memories, but also inviting their spirits to be with us, perhaps whispering wisdom in our dreams. For we moderns, ancestor spirits are supposed to be superstition, but how many of us keep trinkets once owned by others and passed on for "good luck"?

Markings on cave walls also can be appeals to God or the gods, records of dreams and visions, and declarations of membership in the fellowship of the hunt. Rock art images can also be statements of faith, prayers etched in stone with great patience during rituals. Some speculate that the giant geoglyph impressions in the deserts of Peru at Nazca were danced into the ground.

We can speculate on the meanings of rock art long into the night. Robert Hyder, former Superintendent of Mesa Verde National Park, once told me that the best archeology came from faint voices on the wind that you could hear echoing in the canyons when all the tourists had left. The pull of such rudimentary images to inspire us to speculate is the best measure of their power.

The vibrancy of rock art speaks of early man's psyche, unencumbered by television, telephone, the Internet, e-mail, magazines, newspapers, fax machines and books that demand we shut down our senses. Under favorable conditions, oneness with nature, *participation mystique*, becomes normal waking consciousness, and the dream time is always hovering close by. Images etched into stone thousands of years ago by artists with minds on fire with the spirit of the hunt send sparks of primal electricity directly across the gap between minds. Soul-to-soul communication reminds us of the watery language of our dreams, which seem close by here, even if we are not asleep.

Each night we are treated to a show as we swim through a dream time stream of images, snippets of sounds, and nonlinear stories served up by the unconscious. Dream interpretation would be so easy if we received a printout of interpretations every morning! Alas, until that program is written, most dreams will serve us with a steady flow of puzzles to solve. In the Age of Information, when we are flooded with information everywhere we turn, it seems strange that the one universal language we almost never study in school is dreaming.

There is a reason why dreams are seldom rational. The fluid, perplexing, ever changing symbolic nature of dreams reminds us that the universe is a perpetual creative system. Joseph Campbell went so far as to assert that the prevailing spirit of the universe is awe. Linking to that wellspring of creativity is a cornerstone of mental health, but also a realm harboring some fear. Some people might become anxious if trapped in such a cave. Psychologists report that many people these days are terrified by dreams of animals chasing them. Such dreams are often a sign of the price we pay for living in what some call the Age of Anxiety. Most of the time when an animal chases you in a dream it means that by its species, form and behavior, the animal is trying to bring an important message to the dreamer. When we meet a half-human, half-animal creature in the dream time — such as the bear with a man's head, or the man wearing deer antlers — then this signals that we have integrated that instinctual passion and can use it to our advantage.

Inner space explorers, such as Carl Jung, reported that as one goes deeper into the wilderness of the psyche, the images unearthed are that of nature — rocks, rivers, trees, birds, predator and prey, clouds, sun and moon. Each animal symbol of the unconscious represents an intelligence and a power linked with an emotion; this is why the cold-blooded killer in the movies is so often called "weasel" or the feathers of raptor birds find their way into the costumes and insignias of soldiers. Within each of us there is a living zoo of symbols of power. Many psychologists assert that within each of us one of the beasts of the soul, a totem animal, is a symbol that best represents our character and personality. Perhaps the totem animals of hunters are bear, wolves, lions, hawks and wolverines, while nonhunters belong to the deer, rabbits, mice or sheep totem clans. Regardless, whether he or she is the leading character or has a minor supporting role in your psyche, there is a hunting animal in each of us who can take center stage if the need arises.

The sign language of the soul affirms that at our most basic essence we are one with nature. Carl Jung explained the connection between symbolism of the psyche and instinctual energies of the unconscious: "What we properly call instincts are physiological urges, and are perceived by the senses. But at the same time, they also manifest themselves in fantasies and often reveal their presence only by symbolic images. These manifestations are what I call archetypes."[3]

The archetype of the hunter is a predator who lives in the depths of the deepest caverns of the human mind, and is both killer and creator. The drawings on the walls remind us that, ultimately, the hunter hunts himself. This insight subsequently leads the hunter to a second meditation, answering the question, "If I were the hunted, how would I like to be killed?"

> Hunting is the master behavior pattern of the human species. It is the organizing activity which integrated the morphological, physiological, genetic and intellectual aspects of the human organism and the population who comprise our species.
>
> WILLIAM S. LAUGHLIN[4]

The Religious Instinct?

Taking the life of graceful, awesome animals stirs the deepest waters of the psyche. Sadness. Awe. Respect comes as naturally as the next sunrise as these sentiments find their way into the heart, leading to deeper and deeper feelings of reverence for nature, feelings which ultimately become love. The heart is the connecting link between the transcendental realms above and the dirt, flesh and blood of the material world.

With respect, like a lightning bolt, comes another higher calling. Some psychiatrists believe man possesses a religious instinct, an inbred urge that draws one to formulate ethical codes to prevent abuse of powers and affirm the higher values of life. Of this, psychiatrist Marie-Louise von Franz has written: "We only know that in the unconscious, instinctive functioning of higher animals, including man, there is a supernatural or better said, a super-rational awareness of things about which we could not know rationally, and therefore it is very healthy, and very important to pay attention to such impulses."[5]

Years before the writings of Jung, Freud, or von Franz, Henry David Thoreau also spoke of the balance of instinct between mundane and transcendental.

> I found in myself, and still find, an instinct toward a higher, or, as it is named, spiritual life, as do most men, and another toward a primitive rank and savage one, and I reverence them both. I love the wild not less than the good.[6]

Passing a hunter education course covering safety, wildlife biology, and etiquette is required in order to obtain a hunting license nearly everywhere. Requiring these classes has had a significant effect on increasing hunter safety. (It is now safer to walk the woods in deer season than the streets of some large cities.) But usually left unsaid in the instruction is how to take the feelings stirred in the hunt and express them in a meaningful manner that integrates them into the hunter's soul, and preserves the highest values of the spirit of the hunt.

Hunting once was one of the most basic pillars of religion. In Europe, we find some religious hunting customs still very much alive. They are largely unknown elsewhere. In the United States, here and there hunters quietly have developed their own ritual forms and beliefs, but the lack of a socially sanctioned and publicly understood religious context for hunting makes the hunter more vulnerable to criticism from nonhunters. Today, when modern hunting technology makes hunters more potent than ever before, the moral, ethical and religious aspects of hunting are as essential to hunting as arrows are to archery.

Some may feel ill at ease at the mention of ceremony and ritual; this is an area associated with the clergy and churches. Actually, our lives are filled with routines of actions, linked together to create results — rituals. A baseball player, tugging at his cap, shuffling his feet and wagging the bat enacts a performance ritual, like a golfer addressing his ball, or people dressing for success wearing a certain tie or color of underwear. Putting on grandpa's hat, carrying strings of metal bands of birds shot in

INUIT ETCHING. "TWO MEN DISCUSSING THE COMING HUNT" KAVAVOOK, BAKER LAKE INUIT

the past, and tossing out that special old decoy are a small sample of the hunter's many rituals.

Ceremonies invite more people to join in a ritual and mark the specialness of an event to a larger group. Something as simple as a toast, thanking the spirit of the wild for its bounty, can be a ceremony honoring nature and the hunt if it's from the heart.

Properly done, what rituals and ceremonies do is add to the depth of an experience, and ensure that standards of ethics and etiquette are preserved. They create continuity and aid in conserving heritage. One cannot hunt for long and not be drawn to use ceremony and ritual to express the rich feelings only the hunter comes to know. The spirit of the hunt, therefore, is a passionate blend of earthly pragmatism and lofty ethics, philosophy and ceremony.

The Power of Story

The winds howl outside and the flames leap skyward inside. With the ancient images on the walls watching, we could try to spend our time measuring the size and shape of the cave, determining the chemistry of its rock walls, or performing calculations on portable computers. But why? The spirit of the hunter's cave invites, maybe demands us to contemplate more profound matters.

Time and space meld into a kind of flowing oneness as the fire casts its spell. Imagination soars. As the fire burns, contemplating the shapes on the walls, as well as the hunters that pursue them, our mind seems drawn to link symbols together into strings of association. With the aid of brother fire, the forerunner of the television set, we come to realize that man's nature is to be a story-telling animal. This is

how we make sense of things. How can one not create and tell stories in a hunter's cave? Does man have a story-telling instinct, too?

Stories of the hunt are one of the oldest enduring elements of human culture, for good reason. Hunting stories are more than entertainment. Greenland Eskimos believe that it is the responsibility of a hunter to return to the community and tell the stories of his hunt in the greatest detail possible. Hunt stories pass along the wisdom of hunting to future generations, and energize people with the spirit of nature, which is an inspiring, perhaps even healing force.

For many people, the spear, the hook, and the bow and arrow have been replaced by the credit card, the pen and the checkbook when it comes to harvesting meat. Hunting stories represent a touchstone of honesty in a largely sanitized world. It is healthier for the soul to be biologically honest than to be politically correct.

Spending enough time in a hunter's cave makes us ponder the ultimate question: Do we tell the stories, or do they tell us?

To aid our quest for good stories, let us imagine that we are joined by others who feel the pulse of the hunt throb in their veins and have pondered its meanings — a hunting club of sorts. In a technological age, this kind of gathering would be possible with satellites and computers. In earlier times, native hunters assert they achieved the same union of minds at a distance with dream telepathy. Regardless of how such a group is called together, let us now call the meeting to order.

The night is long. The spirit is strong. Let the convocation begin. The first speaker is Dr. Erik Fritzell, chairman of Fisheries and Wildlife at Oregon State University:

When I hunt I am immersed mentally, physically and even spiritually in an age-old predatory relationship among animals. I am participating in a common ecological process — just as a fox seeks her prey. I do not need to kill to eat — although I enjoy and appreciate eating game meat immensely. I kill in order to have hunted. To me, hunting is a very personal relationship between myself, the prey, and the environment in which the chase occurs. When I take my annual pilgrimage to the North Dakota pothole country, I take great pleasure in spending the vast majority of my time seeking just the right place to attempt to kill some ducks. In a sense, I am hunting for an ecosystem in which to participate. This participation, to me, is a form of ecological worship.

For millions of years we survived as hunters. In the few short millennia since our divorce from that necessity, there has been no time for significant bioloical change — anatomical, physiological or behavioral. Today, we have small hope of comprehending ourselves and our world unless we understand that man still, in his innermost being, is a hunter.

ROBERT ARDREY[7]

CHAPTER 2

The Quarry

I never voyaged so far in all my life. You shall see men you never heard of before, whose names you don't know, going away down through the meadows with long ducking guns, with water-tight boots, wading through the fowl meadow grass, on bleak wintry, distant shores, with guns at half-cock; and they shall see teal — blue-winged, green-winged, sheldrakes, whistlers, black ducks, ospreys, and many other wild and noble sights before night, such as they who sit in parlors never dream of.

HENRY DAVID THOREAU

Passionate deer, wily raccoons, governing bears, sly foxes, cold-blooded weasels, lofty geese — animals symbolize our instincts, our identity and our emotions. Within each of us there is a primary animal, a totem that speaks to our true nature, as well as many supporting characters who may take the stage depending on the situations. Ultimately, we are a composite of beasts not unlike an Indian totem pole. In the presence of wild animals, sparks of energy leap across space to remind us of our own animals within.

Towering cedar totem poles may seem to be analogous to religious statues of gods or goddesses. Not really, say the Pacific Northwest coastal Indian tribes. In their world, each person has special unique ties to certain species of animals. These associations are inherited and shared among families like relatives. A totem pole, then, is a little like stating your genealogy extending into the spirit world where people and animals are equals.

Modern science scoffs at such animistic beliefs. But, often one branch of science is not aware of what another is doing. It is now a proven fact that when a person enters a strong electromagnetic field, that in a short time, the inner bioelectrical field of that person will entrain with those in the external field to become more and more harmonious. To be in the presence of wild animals, especially herds, flocks and swarms of wild animals, is to be in contact with a very vital field of energy and spirit. Considering the findings about bioentrainment, what is the consequence of entrainment with an enormous flock of birds?

Ronald Stromstad is a wildlife biologist — the director of operations for the Western Region of the United States for the conservation organization Ducks Unlimited, Inc. His story of an encounter with a cloud of snow geese attests to the numinous power of wild geese.

A Heavenly Encounter

I n spite of growing up in devout Scandinavian Lutheran surroundings, I'm not a deeply religious person. While Mom may remain dismayed by my poor church attendance record, I suspect that at least some of the "rules of life" may have rubbed off on me, sometimes in spite of my best intentions otherwise. However, in 1996, six of us witnessed a spectacle that I have often found difficult to put into words, except as a "religious experience."

The timing of our North Dakota snow goose hunting trip was perfect. It was late October as we set the 1,200 snow goose decoys in the wheat stubble field. The snow fell heavily, and the temperature was only 15 degrees Fahrenheit. An Arctic wind near 30 miles per hour was pushing huge concentrations of waterfowl out of Canada and into northern North Dakota. The resulting migrational phenomena was dubbed the "Grand Passage" by Ducks Unlimited. In fact, the hasty retreat of millions of waterfowl in such a short time caused air traffic control radar operations to malfunction in some of the Midwest airports.

The six of us lying on the frozen ground in the decoys were all wildlife biologists who had chosen waterfowl and wetlands as our area of expertise and focus. We like waterfowl, and we enjoy waterfowl hunting. Mid-continent snow geese populations were already on their rapid ascent, and it wasn't unusual to have one-and-a-half to three million birds staging in North Dakota at one time. Most of the birds can be found staging in the northern tier of counties on three national wildlife refuges, feeding morning and evening in adjacent stubble fields.

The evening prior to the hunt, we scouted the area to find locations where the birds were feeding, knowing that they were most likely

to return to the same area in the morning. About three-quarters of a mile from the refuge boundary, we discovered a quarter section of wheat stubble seemingly covered with snow geese from end to end. Arriving back at the location at 4:30 a.m., we quickly set about the task of setting up our spread, and were lying on the ground in our "whites" by shooting time. We didn't have to wait long for the spectacle of a lifetime.

Our hope was that the geese would leave the refuge in small groups, providing a morning of shooting opportunities. What occurred, however, was the opposite. One of the fellows shouted "Here they come!" and I looked toward the refuge to see a huge concentration of birds headed our way. We later "guesstimated" the flock of snows in the neighborhood of 30,000 to 40,000 birds. As they arrived at our decoy spread, they began milling and circling directly above us, just out of shooting range. The cacophony of sound was nearly deafening as tens of thousands of geese swirled above us at 80 to 100 yards. For the next several moments we were mesmerized by the spectacle. The scene played out in slow motion, but probably lasted only 15 or 20 seconds. Then, convinced that our decoys weren't to be associated with, the birds drifted off and landed in a field nearby.

For the next few moments there was silence in our decoys as we contemplated what we had just observed and heard. Finally, one of my fellow hunters said, "Oh, my God." We got to our feet and quietly shuffled toward a meeting spot in the middle of the decoys. Not much was said. In retrospect, I believe we were afraid of shattering the moment. Other hunters have witnessed such a spectacle, though not a lot of them. As I reflect on those precious seconds of seeing nature in her most glorious splendor, the thought occurs to me that a nonhunter would never have the same opportunity we had to be exposed to our "religious experience."

Animals may be food, but they may also be beautiful, captivating, deities, or masks of a larger God. Native people all around the world consider animals as wise beings. Among the Pawnee tribe of Native American Indians, in 1904, Chief Letakots-Lesa told Natalie Curtis how his people regarded the animals:

> In the beginning of all things, wisdom and knowledge were with the animals: for Tirawa, the One Above, did not speak directly to man. He sent certain animals to tell men that he showed himself through the beasts, and that from them, and from the stars and the sun and the moon, man should learn. Tirawa spoke to man through his works.[1]

From zooplankton on up to whales, the food chain exists on the law "flesh eats flesh." Life as we know it is not possible without hunting. Carnivores and omnivores must kill to live. Even herbivores must kill to live, for plants are alive and have emotions, as modern science has affirmed.

All living things are born with a programmed set of instructions implanted into their genetic code that guide the development of mind and body. Instincts are most likely formed, over time, out of a kind of Darwin's "survival of the fittest" principle of natural selection. Among predators, there must be a hunting instinct. Like other instincts, not only is it functional, but it is also supported by a "carrot" of emotional enjoyment that comes with hunting — what we might refer to as the spiritual ecstasy of the hunt. We share this instinct with countless other predators, perhaps sometimes being inspired by the proficiencies of the raptors, the big cats and the bears who kill with such grace and proficiency.

If hunters come preprogrammed to hunt, what about the prey? What mental set do they inherit from being eaten for countless thousands of years?

If one watches wild animals catch and eat each other, one never sees guilt associated with the kill, even among foxes, bears and members of the weasel family who sometimes run amok in breeding populations of birds, engaging in bloody, ecstatic orgies. Jose Ortega Y Gasset, in his classic work *Meditations On Hunting*, writes that every human hunter feels ill at ease in the depth of his soul at the thought of killing an animal.[2] Guilt is the emotion most likely to strike a hot knife of incrimination into the feeling of satisfaction that comes with the killing shot of the modern hunter. This is probably true for some hunters, although sadness mixed with personal joy is more likely to be the feeling of a seasoned hunter. The native hunter also may feel sadness and respect for animals, but fear, not guilt, is their emotional issue toward killing. They fear that if animals are not respected, killed humanely, and allowed to renew their numbers, not only will food become short, but accidents, injury, illness and misfortune will result as the revenge of nature for upsetting the balance of the food chain.

From all around the world, much the same story is told — in the beginning, prey animals negotiated blood contracts with human predators. Seers, wizards and shamans, who communicate directly with the spirits of animals through dreams and visions, uniformly report that prey animals understand that being killed and eaten is likely. Accepting the reality of their place in the food chain, the animals in turn set down the conditions under which man may hunt and kill them.

There are hundreds of different hunted species, but by far the most widely prized mammals are members of the deer family. Wherever one travels, deer are honored through songs, dances, masks, stories and legends. A universal symbol of passion and fertility, the word for deer flesh — venison — is derived from the ancient times when the deer was seen as the son of the Greek goddess of love, Venus.

In 1971, anthropologist Karl W. Luckert met the esteemed Navajo medicine man Claus Chee Sonny, who was then 71 years old. The shaman had worked with a number of western medical practitioners, but he was best known for his knowledge of a spiritual approach to deer hunting, "The Deer Huntingway." After some consideration, Claus Chee Sonny decided to share his wisdom about the contract between man and deer. The following words are his own. As you read them, notice how at times he speaks as a human, and at other times, his voice changes and it is as if he is a deer. If you asked him, he would say this is because he was chosen to be a voice for the deer spirit, an honor which originated from the choosing of the deer.

Graystreak Mountain

There is a place called Graystreak Mountain *(k'idziibahi)*. It was the time when only the Gods or Holy-people were alive. There were no Navajo yet. Human beings had not been created yet. Graystreak Mountain is the place where the gods live; it looks as though a gray streak of sand extends up the side of the mountain. But the name of the mountain is not derived from its color. It was not named that way because it is gray; rather, it was named after the color of the game animals, such as deer.

Nearby is a house — now a low hill — which was the sweat lodge of the gods. This is the place where they lived; and they would build a fire to make the rocks very hot for the sweat bath. When everybody was about ready to go into the lodge they kept noticing a black person that would come. After everybody had gone inside, the black person would come in. He came in once. He came in twice. And the third time the people started asking: 'Who is he?' 'Where is he from?' 'What is he?'

The fourth time they set a trap for him. The trap was set so that the gods would find out from where and who he was. Two divine persons, Red-Tailed Hawk and Robin, were stationed outside the sweat lodge to watch for the black person. (Inside the gods were singing sweat lodge songs by Talking-god.)

The black person alighted at the peak of Graystreak Mountain. The place where he sat down is called 'Home of Lightning.' The gods, not man, gave this name. Therefore this mountain is sacred.

Then he started flying again and sat down by the sweat lodge. He took his coat and simply stepped out of it. It was Black-god appearing in the form of Crow. That is why this person was black. He is a big man, and he simply took off his coat and went inside.

So they all had gone into the sweat lodge. They came out once. They came out twice. They came out three times. The fourth time he did not go back in. But, the two persons who were stationed saw him put his black coat back on. When he had put on his coat he started flying east and went up above the cliff. He headed back in the same direction from where he had come, toward Navajo Mountain. The two persons who were stationed watched him. They discovered where the black person lives and later told what happened.

After they had gone into the sweat lodge for the fourth time, the people decided that one of them should be transformed into a little puppy. Then the people moved southward and left the little Puppy in the ashes of their extinct campfire. The little dog was instructed: 'Watch your eyes when he starts pecking! But do allow him to pick you up!' Then the people moved and left the little Puppy in the ashes.

Crow came to the little dog and began pecking him. And the Puppy howled and cried, and all the while avoided being pecked in the eyes. Crow picked him up. He carried the Puppy out toward the east and in the direction of Navajo Mountain. Disappearing behind that mountain, he came back out and flew back to Black Mountain. He landed on the highest peak of Black Mountain, on Rim Hill (*adaahwiidzoh*). This peak looks a little like a Red Ant Hill. It is the house of the black person — the home of Black-god.

Behind the door, inside the house, all the game animals were kept. No animal was left in the surface world, because Black-god had herded them all into his house. All game animals, large and small, were in his house. All game animals belong to him. It is today as it was then.

The doorkeeper is Porcupine. He is also called A-messy-object-in-a-tree, Old Buckskin, and Grinding-stone. He has a turquoise rod, a stick that is used for stirring fires. By using this rod, poking straight on forward, he split the door open. And he threw the Puppy in; then he left to go somewhere. When he returned he took the Puppy back out of the house. Having thus freed him, Porcupine no longer paid any attention. But then, Puppy, who was actually a strong man, punched Porcupine in the nose. He knocked him out. Then he did exactly what the gatekeeper had done earlier to open the gate. He took the turquoise rod, poked it straight, and so split the gate open. The gate opened. Inside he saw game animals, located in all the four directions — east, south, west and north.

And the animals began escaping through the open gate. The jackrabbits, cottontails, chipmunks, and squirrels. All these were among the animals whom Black-god had herded into his house. And all the animals came out of the gate while the gatekeeper was lying unconscious on the side.

The first four deer, all from the same family, came running through the gate. The Puppy touched them between their legs. Of all the other animals who came running after them he touched the nose. This is what made them sensitive to odors. The Puppy touched the animals on the tip of the ears, the tip of the tail, and the tips of their hair. He, for that purpose, was being picked up by whatever it was, touched them at their ears, at the tip of the tail, and at the tips of their hair, and at their noses too. The wind was used to touch the animals with. This is why the animal knows and hears what is coming before he sees it.

The animal can hear you, even when you just start out to hunt him. That is why you

Navajos emerging from sweat lodge, circa 1960.

never should talk in a manner of which the deer would disapprove. So, whenever you hunt, the animal knows what you want. He is dressed in wind; because the Puppy touched him with wind all over the body, and because he touched his nose and made him sensitive to smell.

The animals escaped across the plain. In a northward loop they took the direction of Graystreak Mountain. The Puppy followed them and caught up with them. But the animals were scared of him. They smelled him and they heard him in the wind. They would not come near him. So he went back to his friends. This is the story, the story of releasing game animals who were kept from the people. The person was transformed into a puppy for that purpose.

The Quarry

After they had been released from Black-god's house, a song was given to the game animals. With this song, with two kinds of lightning, with rainbow, and with the roots of sunlight they were to travel across the prairie. In this manner all the animals, different kinds of deer, lions, buffalo, all traveled across the prairie — kicking up dust and knocking branches off the plants. This dust and these plants are used today as medicine. I use it every once in a while. And so it is. Now I give you the song with which the animals traveled across the prairie. With the above-mentioned four means of travel and with this song they crossed the prairie:

Ah'eh na-ya-ya-ya.
I walk on an invisible arch (repeat), na-ya-ya.
I walk on an invisible arch (repeat), na-ya-ya.
I am the son of him who blends with the white earth,
I walk on an invisible arch, I walk on . . ., na-ya-ya.
From the top of White mountain,
I walk on an invisible arch, I walk on . . ., na-ya-ya.
The son of the Female Wind,
I walk on an invisible arch, I walk on . . ., na-ya-ya.
With a bow in my hand,
I walk on an invisible arch, I walk on . . ., na-ya-ya.
With a feathered arrow in my hand,
I walk on an invisible arch, I walk on . . ., na-ya-ya.
The Female Wind with sensitive ears,
I walk on an invisible arch, I walk on . . ., na-ya-ya.

With my feet ready to go anywhere,
I walk on an invisible arch, I walk on . . ., na-ya-ya.
Ready to go any time of the day,
I walk on an invisible arch, I walk on . . ., na-ya-ya.
As the son of Light Feather,
I walk on an invisible arch. I walk on . . ., na-ya-ya.
I walk on an invisible arch, I walk on (four times) . . . na-ya-ya.

[Claus Chee Sonny called attention to the ending of the song, saying that according to the deer gods, "The ending of this song is always 'yeh!', never a timid 'ya.' Because if someone hits us with an arrow, the sound of our fall is always 'yeh!' The end of deer life and of a deer hunting song is the same, always 'yeh!'"

According to Navajo tradition, hunting-way songs are sung before the hunt, in a sweat lodge. During the hunt, one speaks little, often in a special language, and only prayers are offered. When the hunt is concluded, then another sweat lodge may be held, and hunting songs may again be sung.]

With this song the game animals arrived at Graystreak Mountain. Over that mountain the animals still come into the valley at night; toward morning they return to the mountains beyond. So, early in the morning you see a gray streak moving up the side of the mountain. Between Graystreak Mountain and the above-mentioned sweat lodge lies a narrow ravine. Right there the next episode of the story took place.

Deer Huntingway

In the ravine, where Graystreak Mountain and the Sweat Lodge face each other, the man who earlier had been a puppy waited in ambush. Wind had told him: "There is where the tracks are. The deer will come marching through there in a single file.í There were not guns yet then; only bows and arrows were used to hunt. The hunter had four arrows — one was made of sheet lightning, one of zigzag lightning, one of sunlight roots, and one of rainbow. These are the four types of arrows which also the friends of this man had.

The Large Buck

Then the first deer, a large buck, came with many antlers. The hunter got ready to shoot the buck. His arrow was in place. But, just as he was ready to shoot, the deer had transformed himself into a mountain mahogany bush. After a while a mature man stood up from this bush. He stood up and said, 'Do not shoot! We are your neighbors. These are things that will be in the future when human beings have come into existence. This is the way you will kill us. And this is the way you will eat us.' And he told the hunters how to kill and eat the deer. So the hunter let the mature Deer-man go at the price of his information. And the Deer-man left.

The Doe

Then the large doe, a shiny doe, appeared behind the one who had left. The hunter was ready again, to shoot the doe in the heart. But the doe turned into a cliffrose bush ("bitter bush" Purshia tridentata). A while later a young woman stood up from the bush. The woman said, 'Do not shoot! We are your neighbors. In the future when man has been created, men will live because of us. Men will use us to live on.' So then, at the price of her information, the hunter let the Doe-woman go. And so she left.

The Two-Pointer

Then a young buck, a two-pointer, came along. And the hunter got ready to shoot the two-pointer. But the deer transformed himself into a dead tree. After a while, a young man stood up from the dead tree and said, '—- in the future, after man has been created, if you talk about us in the wrong way, we will cause trouble for you if you urinate, and we will trouble your eyes. We will trouble your ears if we do not approve of what you say about us.' And so at the price of this information, the hunter let the young Deer-man go.

The Fawn

Then the little Fawn appeared. The hunter was ready to shoot the Fawn, but the Fawn turned into a lichen-spotted rock. After a while, a young girl stood up from the rock and spoke: 'In the future all this will happen if we approve; and whatever we shall disapprove shall all be up to me. I am in charge of all the other deer people. If you talk bad about us, and if we disapprove of what you say, I am the one who will respond by killing you. I will kill you with what I am. If you hear the cry of my voice, you will know that trouble is in store for you. If you do not make use of us properly, even in times when we are numerous, you will not see us anymore. We are the four deer who have transformed themselves into different kinds of things. Into these four kinds of things we can transform ourselves. Moreover, we can assume the form of all the different kinds of plants. Then, when you look you will not see us. In the future, only those of whom we approve shall eat the mighty deer. If, when you hunt, you come across four deer, you will not kill all of them. You may kill three and leave one. But if you kill us all, it is not good.'

This is what the little Fawn said — that,

what he is, is not good. 'Where I go, before me travel snowstorms. All other things too, which are no good, go in front of me. This is my protection. If you are walking on an unused road and see the tracks of a doe, or if a doe catches up with you from behind, that is I. And knowing of this you will not bother me.

These are things which will bring you happiness. When you kill a deer, you will lay him with the head toward your house. You will cover the earth with plants or with branches of trees, lengthwise, with the growing tips of the plants pointing the direction of the deer's head — toward your house. So it shall be made into a thick padding, and the deer shall be laid on that. Then you will take us home to your house and eat of us. You will place our bones under any of the things whose form we can assume — mountain mahogany, cliff rose, dead tree, lichen-spotted rock, spruce, pine, or under any of the other good plants. At these places you may put our bones. You will sprinkle the place with yellow pollen. Once. Twice. Then you will lay the bones. And then you will sprinkle yellow pollen on top of the bones. This is for the protection of the game animals. In this manner they will live on; their bones can live again and live a lasting life.'

This is what the little Fawn told the hunter. 'You will be able to use the entire body of the deer, even the skin. And we belong to Talking-god. We belong to Black-god. We are in his hand. And he is able to make us deaf and blind. Those among you, of whom he approves, are the good people. They will hunt with success and be able to kill us. According to his own decisions he will surrender us to the people. The Black-god is Crow.

But when you hunt you do not refer to him as Crow but as Black-god. Today, still, the game animals belong to Talking-god and Black-god.

So these are the four who gave information. Man was created later. All these events happened among the gods, prior to the creation of man. All animals were like human beings then, they were able to talk. Thus, this story was not made up by old Navajo men. These events were brought about by Black-god."

The hunter let the four magic deer go, and he followed them. They showed him many things, about plants, stones, special places, and other animals, so the story goes. Finally the deer gods passed on a song, which when sung, supposedly attunes the hunter with Talking-god and Black-god so their actions will be in accord with what is right. This song goes:

Ah'eh na–ya–ya.

Early in the morning you can see me (three times) na–ya–ya.

The Yellow Hawk can see us, na–ya–ya.

The Male Rain can see us, na–ya–ya.

The Black Bow can see us, na–ya–ya.

The Eagle-Feathered Arrow can see us, na–ya–ya.

All arrows that fit your bow can see us, na–ya–ya.

The Arrow-which-hits-the-heart can see us, na–ya–ya.

Early in the morning you can see us, na–ya–yeh!

The four deer of the Navajo Deer Huntingway: a big buck, a forkhorn, a doe and a fawn

Final Instructions

All of the deer gods, who lived at the beginning, went into the hole at the south side of Black Mountain; through it they returned underground to the house of their origin — to the home of Black-god, which is the peak of Black Mountain. All the wild deer, which are now available, come from either the mountain mahogany bush or the other things into which deer can transform themselves. Concerning the way in which men are expected to hunt them, the divine Deer-people gave these final instructions:

You should never point an arrow or a gun at just anything. If you point your weapon unnecessarily, the deer simply turns into whatever you happen to aim at. If you walk over to it, you find plants and rocks, but not us. So you should always hold onto your weapon tightly. Because if it starts slipping away from your hand, you will only send us away. So do not play around.

You should not talk bad about us game animals when you hunt. We can hear you, even over a moutain. And if you find us in numbers of four, you may not kill all of us. You must leave one.

In winter, when you think you have hunted sufficient meat to last you till spring, when you kill a male deer last, you can take a whisker of the deer and throw it to the east. You call the deer by his name and pray what you wish to pray — then the hunting season is over. If you happen to kill a female deer as your last one, you do the same, except you throw the whisker to the west; pray what you have to pray, and close the season.

You will not throw the bones away just anywhere. Everything of which we are made, such as our skin, meat, bones, is to be used. They are most useful. And this is true. Anything that we hold on to, such as earth from the four sacred mountains, the rainbow, the jewels, the corn,

all the plants we eat, will be in us. Our bodies contain all these. And because of this we are very useful. Our very bones can be useful for making white needles. Needles can be made from the bones of the front legs and the hind legs. The ends can be sharpened to a needle-point. This is what we use to stitch buckskins together — and the buckskin is most useful. The usefulness of the deer is the foundation which has been laid; it serves as an example of other things. This is what is meant when we say that the deer are first in all things. We are in the gods who are mentioned, in the mountains, in the rainbows, in the roots of sunlight, in the lightnings. And so we are the most useful thing under the sun. For this reason, an unwounded buckskin — of a deer not killed by a weapon — shall be used in sacred ceremonies. Also, we are in all the plants. In this manner, even the insects are associated with us. And so the buckskins, the white needles, and the meat are first — nowadays even the fat is hard to get. All the meat is very useful. You can put deer meat as medicine on sheep, on horses, and on other domestic animals. All livestock lives because of the deer. That is what keeps the animals moist, breathing, walking about, and altogether alive. And animals are our food. They are our thoughts.

Now this is the way in which the one who holds us in his hands, Talking-god, controls us; Talking-god is first; Black-god (Crow) is next in line; then follow Red-tailed Hawk; then Little Hawk; then Robin. So these, in that order, are the five who control us. These are the ones who put us on the earth, who still give us life. In addition there is Wind, the one who informs the deer at the tips of their ears.

The Talking-god and the Black-god are not to be mentioned in the presence of women and children. [Claus Chee Sonny later said that anyone who has the courage to take this seriously can speak of this and study it with respect.] Their names are to be spoken only when you are out hunting or when you are praying.

If you do everything right, if you remind your hunter companions to hunt properly, you will always have enough to eat. It does not matter how many people there are. You will always get enough if you hunt right, if you prepare the animals correctly, if you bring them home properly, and if you dispose of the bones in the proper manner. And this is true today. If you follow this advice of the Deer-people, you will always get enough to eat. But if you do wrong, if against the rules you urinate on the bones even on the hair of the deer, you will be troubled when you urinate.

The Talking-god advises you not to tamper with the head of the deer. If you do, then either a young child, or a young girl, or a young woman in the family will become blind or deaf. Both Talking-god and Black-god advise you not think anything bad about the game animals, that you do not follow the same pattern as you do when you slaughter a sheep. You will not cut the throat. If you butcher a deer like you butcher a sheep, you will become insane and you will get lost somewhere.

These rules were not made by men. They were made by the gods before the creation of humankind. These rules must be kept sacred.

These rules were made so that man would be able to reach old age without losing his hearing and without losing his eyesight.

. . . Men will have a difficult time hunting us. While they may see us, we can turn into another object. Their eyes will follow us but we will disappear. If a man is out hunting, we can stand nearby in such a manner that he may shoot all his arrows at us. He runs out of arrows. Finally he will go home and say, 'I did not get any,' or he may say, 'I do not know what they were.' This is because when man started to hunt, he started with the wrong attitude. That is why he did not get any.

If we waggle our tails, you may not bother us. If we stop to urinate, you may not interrupt us. If we wiggle our ears, you will not bother us; you will only look at us and search for another one of us.

Then the deer pointed to the other one, the Ice-god. He is the one who is able to stand before the hunter without being struck down. He can stand there for you to shoot at, but you will run out of arrows — because there is nothing in the buckskin. An empty buckskin will appear before you, and you will waste all your arrows shooting at it. And the body will go back into the buckskin after you have run out of arrows, and will run away. That is the way it will be with Ice-god.

So it is clear now what the deer gods have communicated. It is something important. It should be taken seriously and kept sacred." [3]

Similar beliefs of the spiritual nature of animals are held by the Koyukon, an Indian tribe of Alaska, reports anthropologist Richard Nelson. He writes: "Traditional Koyukon people live in a world that watches, in a forest of eyes. . . [where] the natural and supernatural worlds are inseparable, and environmental events are often caused or influenced by spiritual forces." The central figure in the Koyukon pantheon of nature spirits is Raven, who created all things. Another mask of black god.

Koyukons see each person as having a symbol that best expresses their identity, an archetype, so to speak. When Yukon River Koyukon Indians want to know about the nature of a person, they may ask, "What animal is he?" [4]

Mexican deer dance mask:Cora or Tarajumara tribe.

Chapter 3

Invoking the Gods

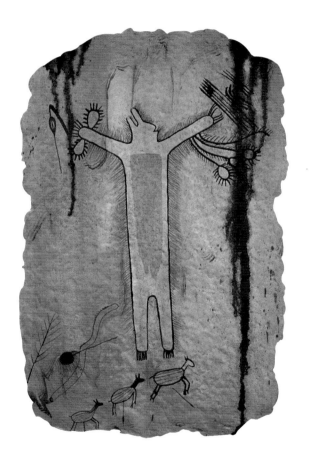

In every civilized man was a pagan waiting to come out,
who really believed in the gods of the mountains,
and in appeasing the spirits of dead game.

Tom Clancy, Rainbow Six, 1998[1]

Considering the short time actually spent hunting each year by the average hunter — about a week — and the amount of time spent planning for those precious hunting days, one is forced to conclude that preparation is as important to hunting as a cloud is to rain. Planning, scouting, reading magazines and books, fixing gear, practicing, buying equipment, visiting expositions — the modern hunter is not unlike the traditional Hopi Indian who is said to have spent as much as 75 percent of his life either participating in rituals or preparing for them. Like the Hopis, there are spiritual aspects at all stages of the hunt. Garnering their favor has been a concern since the earliest of times:

> *. . . I declare that no human activity turns out well without the help of the gods . . . So men who are interested in hunting should not neglect Artemis of the wild, or Apollo, or Pan, or the Nymphs, or Hermes, god of the ways and pathfinder, or any other god of the mountains . . . One must believe . . . and begin every activity, including hunting, with the gods.*
>
> ARRIAN OF NICOMEDIA
> (CIRCA 136 AD)[2]

Despite all the enjoyable elements, hunting is serious business. Hunters take chances, face danger, risk injury and use lethal weapons. By nature, a hunter assumes responsibility for the life of animals. Unnecessary suffering is not an option for an ethical hunter. The more deadly serious a hunter is, the more he enjoys what he's doing.

Offering prayers and perhaps even making a simple sacrifice — such as scattering a few grains of corn meal and invoking each of the four directions of the compass, the worlds above and below, as well as the middle world where we live — are ways that hunters, modern and traditional, ask for God's guidance, support and protection. Others recite a favorite passage from The Bible or pound out a rhythm on a moose skin drum. Some simply stop, let the experience soak in, and recognize how lucky they are to be doing this.

There is great diversity in the ways that hunters ask for the gods to be with them in the hunt. Comparing and contrasting the traditions of the world, one cannot help but conclude that it's not so much to whom you pray, or how, but what's in your heart when you pray that counts. As Joseph Campbell observes: "The gods and goddesses then are to be understood as embodiments and custodians of the elixir of Imperishable Being but not themselves the Ultimate in its primary state. What the hero seeks through his intercourse with them is therefore not finally themselves, but their grace, i.e., the power of their sustaining substance."[3]

A SAAMI SEIDDE, OR SACRIFICE STONE

Stones are heavy physical objects that anchor spiritual sentiments to earthly reality. All around the world one of the most common altars is a stone set at a special place to honor a divine presence. In northern Scandinavia, the Saami people (or Lapps) place stones known as *Seidde* at special places, marking them as holy. The origins of the word *Seidd*e are two-fold: a hunting territory of a group, and that of a spirit, a guardian of the place. The stone is not the spirit, but a marker of the presence of the spirit. *Seidde* are commonly erected in mountain areas or along the shores of lakes where some supernatural event is said to have taken place.

To show respect for the gods, the Saami would traditionally sacrifice a reindeer at a *Seidde*. A popular god honored in this fashion was *Stoorjunckare* (The Vice Regent of God), who is the master of the birds and of the fish. *Stoorjunckare* is said to show himself to people in the shape of a man dressed in beautiful Norwegian clothing, but with the feet of a bird. He is supposed to give good luck to bird hunters and fishermen. When a Saami shaman, *Noaidi*, would make a sacrifice to appeal for luck in hunting bigger game, it is generally believed that he would address his prayers to the bear, which was the mediator between man and the animals.[5]

A Saami hunter would offer a prayer at the Seidde, or back home in the village at shrines located behind their huts. The following is such a prayer recorded in the early 1800s:

Soften, forest, moisten
  woods yield, dear Tapio
  be kind, world of gods.
As a man goes to hunt
be gracious. Forest Mistress
careful maid of Tapiola,
  open the wide shed
  break your lock of bone
  let the quarry run
  along golden paths
  along silver roads!
Ukko, it will only be
you if you give me a sign;
  drive your game, O God,
  round it up yourself.[6]

SAAMI DRUMMER AND SAAMI DRUM

HUICHOL INDIAN YARN PAINTING:
The Huichol Indians of Mexico consider the deer spirit Kauyumari to be the guiding spiritual force for their religion and culture. Shooting an arrow in a Huichol yarn painting can have more than one meaning. It can depict a deer hunt, or it can also be a symbolic statement of a prayer (represented by the arrow) being sent to Kauyumari.

RIGHT: WHITE DEERSKIN DANCE, HOOPA TRIBE, CIRCA 1900
Among the Indians of Northern California, the White Deerskin Dance is an annual ceremony of renewal performed in late summer. Deer are seen as mythic, symbols of creativity and vessels of communication between gods and man. Donning white deerskins, the dancers are said to embody the spirit of deer.

Following an appropriate invocation, the hunter might then ask the gods for guidance. The answer, if any at all, could come in a wide variety of ways, often with the same metaphoric language of dreams. While there are many oracular methods — dreams, visions, interspecies communication with animals, tossed stones or bones, etc. — a common Saami tradition was to use a special divining drum whose skin was decorated with a number of animals and spirits. Using a piece of reindeer antler for a beater, the hunter would sing a rhythmic chant called a *joik*, accompanying himself on the drum. A ring, often made of brass, would be placed on the drum. The ring would bounce up and down as the *joik* was being performed. At the conclusion of the chant, the final position of the ring was believed to be a message from the gods about species of animals to pursue, and the right time and place to hunt.

Spiritual Beings Governing and Guiding the Hunt

Hunting is presided over by deities of all sorts: animals, spirits, saints, ascended ancestors, mythic and legendary beings, as well as a single divine being or intelligence that oversees all else. Some cultures directly worship animals as gods or embodiments of spirits. Among the Ainu of Japan, bears are representatives of the god *Kamui*, who also presides over hunting.

The guiding spirit of the Huichol Indians of Mexico is Kauyumari, the deer. Living in high mountains, and traveling long distances on foot over steep terrain, it would be wise to identify with the deer for inspiration, rather than, say, the turtle or the lizard. While the deer is a major deity, Huichols do hunt and kill deer. This is in keeping with anthropologist Weston LaBarre's observation that, "The first religion was to kill God and eat him."

Black God, embodied in the crow, is the Navajo Indian spirit guide of the hunt. Further north among the Koyukon Indians of Alaska, the raven is the presiding spirit. In

South America, a hunter might regard a condor as a hunter's god, while in Africa, an eagle might serve the same value. Places, rivers, stones, and caves may also have presiding spirits. Gods of the hunt come in all sizes, shapes, colors and forms. In general, male deities aid the hunter's strength, endurance, skills and luck. Goddesses provide fertility and abundance for those who give both them and nature proper respect. They punish transgressions with illness, bad fortune and scarcity.

The origins of both sacrifice and sacrament, two foundations of religious worship in all traditions, were originally associated with hunters' prayers to create proper relationships with the gods in order to obtain their blessings and guidance, and secure protection from evil. In return for proper respect, hunters believed that the gods would send them representatives as animals to be killed and eaten.

Some Gods and Goddesses of the Hunt

Female Goddesses
   CENTRAL AMERICA — Loa, Aḥ Uaynih, Ix Chel, Xmucane
   EAST AFRICA — Masai Moon Goddess
   EASTERN EUROPE — Almoshi, Devana, Vir-ava
   EGYPT — Bast, Mut, Seknet, Thoeris
   FAR EAST — Feng Po, Pang Niang, Guzi, Xi Wangmu
   GREECE — Artemis, Daphne, Kallisto, Melanion, Circe
   HIMALAYAS — Black Vixen-Headed One, Red Snow-bear-headed One, Greenish-black Leopard-headed Great Goddess, Red Tiger-headed One
   INDIA — Shakuntala
   INUIT (polar) — Sedna
   NEAR EAST — Cybele, Gula, Sister Fire, Thitmanat
   NORTH AMERICA — Badger Old Woman, Buffalo Girl, White Buffalo Woman, Moon Woman, Corn Mother
   NORTHERN EUROPE — Frau Gode, Skogsjungfru, Wilden Wip, Gebjon
   OCEANIA — Ai Tupua'i, Po ne'a'aku, Uli, Wibalu
   SOUTH AMERICA — Cocamama, Senhora Ana, Taue Si, Caipora
   SOUTHEAST ASIA — Chitsa Numjan, Pyek Kha Yeh Ki, Yu Kantang
   WEST AFRICA — Oshun (Yoruba - fertility)
   WESTERN EUROPE — Achtan, Brigid, Dea Artia, Minerva Medica, Lahe, Sadb, Fuwch Gyfeilioru, Visuna

Male Gods
   ASIA (Udmurt) — Forest Uncle
   FINLAND — Tapio (Lord of the Forests)
   GREECE — Orion, Aktaion, Hippolytos, Aristaois, Agreus, Pan
   INDIA — Dushyanta
   JAPAN (Ainu) — Kamui (nature spirits)
   MEXICO (Huichol) — Kauyumari, the deer
   NAVAJO (American Indian) — Black God (ravens and crows)
   NIGERIA — Sango
   SCANDINAVIA (Saami) — Stoornjuncke (spirit of forest, Vice Regent of God),Laeik-olmai (hunting god), Leibolmai (alder man who protects bears)
   SUMERIA — Dumuzi
   WEST AFRICA — Ogun, the hunter, and Ochosi, the tracker (Yoruba religion)
   WESTERN EUROPE — Saint Hubert, patron saint of hunting (Christian)

Gods and goddesses are the building blocks from which mankind forms the religions and mythologies that give a sense of meaning, order and wonder to life, as well as establish a sense of moral and ethical standards. Religions and mythologies change in accordance with the times and the needs of people, as well as the fertile creativity of the human mind, which forever is fashioning new numinous symbols to energize and organize consciousness. To anchor religious sentiments, people often associate certain places with strong spirits, gods, goddesses and myths, such as Mt. Olympus in Greece, home to all the Greek gods including those that preside over the hunt, principally Orion and Artemis. Mt. Katahdin in Maine, according to the Penobscot Indians, is the home of Pomola, who has the body of a man, the wings of an eagle, and the head of a moose. Pomola is said to preside over the weather of that region, with the aid of a spirit helper — the storm bird — who warns travelers of impending storms with tiny puffs of wind that come out of stillness.

Among traditional cultures there is a nearly universal belief that once, very long ago, animals could walk and talk, coexisting with man as equals, and communicating with a common language that is often referred to as the language of the birds. Because the normal dimensions of time and space melt away in dreams and visions, it is believed that man can reenter this time to converse with the spirits, just as vitally as the ancestors did.

A common lesson brought out of that dream time is that the animals of each species are interconnected by an invisible spider web of consciousness that not only links all members of that species together, but also is ultimately linked with spirit beings in another dimension who preside over the wisdom and powers of that animal. These powers in turn can be transferred to humans who earn the favor of the spirit beings. Among the Kwakiutl Indians of British Columbia, it is believed that the souls of departed great hunters are reborn into killer whales.

The Inuit Goddess at the Bottom of the Sea

Some legends say that she was an aging widow. Others insist that she was the daughter of a

TALELAYU BY CAPE DORSET INUIT ARTIST KENOJUAK ASHEVAK (1979)

powerful chief. Dozens of variations of her tale have been told and sung in tundra igloos and skin tents. All seem to agree that, once upon a time long ago, there was a time of great famine. All the people climbed into their skin boats — *kayaks* and larger *oomiaks* — to embark on a journey to a new land where they could find food. Regardless of her identity, there was neither enough room nor food for the last woman. As the boats pulled out to sea, she clung steadfast to the side of one of them. To keep the boat from capsizing, the chief had to cut off her fingers, and she quickly slipped under the sea.

Her fingers transformed into seals, sea lions, walruses and whales. In death, she became a powerful Inuit goddess of fertility who presides over the sea creatures and influences the weather. Sedna, Nuliajuk, Arnakaepshaluk, and Talelayu are some of her names; in all subcultures, she is known as the woman at the bottom of the sea. When she is pleased, she sends animals to hunters who show proper respect for animals killed. When eating the flesh of sea mammals, one links with the goddess, and she is able to detect if people do not honor the animals whose lives have been sacrificed to feed them.

Talelayu can be cruel to those who do not show proper reverence for her and the animals. Scarcity, sickness, foul weather and misfortune are the ways she reprimands those who are unfaithful. Inuit believe that, more than any other spirit, she controls the fortune of men.

The first game biologists were shamans, magico-religious practitioners who could enter into altered states of consciousness, as in dreams, visions, and trances, and undertake journeys to other worlds to enlist the aid of spirits. According to tradition, the *angakok*, or Inuit shaman, journeys to visit Talelayu, combs her hair, and does favors for her, and she in turn sees that hunters find seals, whales, and walruses.

The woman at the bottom of the sea is an appropriate fertility deity to a culture that relies so heavily on sea mammals. Inuit are the greatest hunters of all; they must be, for in many areas where they live all food comes from sea mammals. If they avoid illness or injury, some Inuit live to ripe old ages, seemingly in violation of modern dietary advice about a balanced diet, cholestrol and fat. First, remember that they live in a very cold climate and burn off fat quickly. Second, while no plant life can grow on an ice pack, their source of edible plants comes from the stomachs of animals that graze on sea plants that they kill. Seeking a parallel theme among the mythic motifs of females goddesses of the hunt and protectress of animals one could say that the counterpart of Talelayu is Artemis among Greeks; Diana to Romans; and White Buffalo Calf Woman among northern plains Indians.

Hunters In The Stars

In addition to linking special places on earth with spiritual and mythic beings, it seems human nature to associate divine forms with the heavens. Nightly, the hunters' stars in the constellations of Orion and Sagittarius pass overhead. The pole star constellations that we call the Big Dipper have an earlier name of Ursa Major, or the "great bear." In Scandinavia, the Saami look to the same group of stars clustered around the northern pole that we see, but they see different mythic figures. The North Star they call the Pillar of the World. The Big Dipper to them is the Bow and Arrow, held by Favadna (who we call Arcturus), who is shooting at a giant moose that is formed by the stars Cassiopeia, Perseus, and Auriga. What we call the Milky Way is a flock of birds — known as Bird's Ladder — which predicts annual snowfall and the severity of winter. The Pleides are a herd of reindeer calves.

The bushmen of South Africa, who are among the world's greatest hunters, believe the souls of departed human hunters become stars.

According to Laurens Van Der Post, a bushmen elder named Dabé once told him about the hunters in the skies:

At [my] mention of the Sip Wells [a sacred place], the magic home of Oeng-Oeng, and ... [a] brief recapitulation of some of the great themes of his race, the tension between us snapped. His eyes brightened, ... and he said, "Yes. Oh, yes! Yes! Yes! It is true: the stars are hunters."

"All the stars?" I asked, my heart beating faster.

He paused for just a second, then it all came out at length. "Yes! They were all hunters, great hunters, but some were greater than others. For instance there was that star there!" He raised his thin old arm to point with a long finger at the brightest star in the Great Dipper ... That star, he said, was a great hunter who hunted in far away dangerous places in the shape of a lion. Could I not see how fierce its eyes shone and hear the distant murmur of its roar? And there was even one greater! He pointed out Sirius, the star of the dog, at the head of the belted and nimble Orion ... He shook his head vigorously. The greatest hunter was not there yet. It hunted in the darkest and most dangerous places of all, so far away that we could not see it yet. We could see it only in the early morning when it came nearer on its way home.

There was a hunter, a hunter for you! The old father made a lively whistling sound of wonder at the greatness of the hunter. Yes, just before dawn one could see him striding over the horizon, his eye bold and shining, an arrow ready in his bow. When he appeared, the night whished around to make way for him, the red dust spurting at his black heels. He broke off and shook his gray old head, as he once more uttered that sound of wonder, before asking as if the thought had just come to him: "But can't you hear for yourself the cries of the hunt going on up there?"

I assured him I could. He gave a grunt of satisfaction and leaned back on his elbows with a look on his face as if to say, "Well then! There is nothing more to be said about it."[7]

Artemis and Orion

In European tradition, looking toward the heavens we see constellations named to honor the Greek gods of the hunt: Artemis, protector of wild animals, and her suitor, Orion, the mighty hunter. Their story is tragic, like so many Greek myths that constantly warn about the dangers of excess. Artemis and Orion were in love, but Artemis' brother Apollo was jealous of the affection his sister was showing for Orion. One day, when Orion went for a swim, Apollo challenged Artemis to shoot an arrow and hit a small dark object in the ocean a great distance away. Artemis took up the bet and struck the object, which she later learned was Orion when his dead body washed ashore. Stricken with grief and guilt, to honor her lover, she placed him in the skies, along with his dogs, Canis Major and Canis Minor, who eternally hunt for Lepus (the rabbit) and Taurus (the bull).

In modern scientific society, we commonly rationalize mythic tales as purely quaint literature. They are not. Dr. Mary Zeiss Stange, author and associate professor of Religion and Women's Studies at Skidmore College, relates in her story, "When Artemis Smiles," how she sees the mythic image of Artemis as a guiding force to her as a hunter:

Artemis, whom the Greeks knew as goddess of the hunt and of childbirth, is a paradoxical figure. Because she so aptly embodies the painful truth of life's dependence upon death, it is tempting to see only one or the other side of her. On the light side, she is Lady of the Wild Things, of all that is free and unfettered. This Artemis is the rough-and-tumble eternally youthful tomboy, the nurturing protectress of young vulnerable life, the serene moon guiding travelers on their way, the graceful leader of her corps of forest nymphs, dancing in celebration of the life force. In her darker aspect, however, this same Artemis is a bloodthirsty goddess. She is the impersonal death-dealer, destroyer of beauty and innocence. She uses tricks and snares in her dismal craft. She demands animal, even human, sacrifice and is often harshest toward those most ardently devoted to her. It is almost as if she kills them for her sport.

It is all there in her mythology. But the Greeks would have sagely cautioned what too many of us moderns too readily try to forget: that if you have either Artemis, the light or the dark, then you must have both. She is the goddess of the boundary situations, when we are most acutely aware of how thin the margin is between life and death, how the one feeds off the other. A hunter, she dwells, as all hunters do, on the edge of things.

Something else the Greeks understood better than we do: the gods do not "represent" or "symbolize" elements of our world—they are our world. Artemis, the human encounter with life-death-life process, is all nature and all complexity. By day, the shaft-showering goddess roves the mountains with her nymphic hunting companions, slaying lion and boar, hare and hind. In the cool of the evening, with those same companions, in those same mountain meadows, she dances the round-dance of vibrant life, of birth, and bounty and fruition. Artemis takes as she gives, with even-handedness and grace. But she insists we receive her gifts with unflinching awareness of their violent price, knowing that they come wrapped in that tissue-thin membrane between pleasure and pain, that they occur within that microsecond between life and death surrounding the first or final heartbeat.

* * *

Thanksgiving morning, 5 a.m., frosty and overcast. I look skyward, my eyes adjusting to the darkness and my body to the cold. Immediately above me, a round break appears in the clouds, the near-full moon precisely centered, shining through Artemis — Sister Moon, Sister Hunter. Breathing deep now, eyes wide open, I know this will be a good morning.

It is shortly after daybreak when I see my buck. Mine. Poised on a soft-sloping hillside, he is taking in the morning calm with a smaller male companion. Robust young mule deer at the end of the rut, they are full of themselves and completely unaware of me. My buck waits, patiently if unknowingly, as I move as near as I can. When I pull the trigger, he falls instantly. The other deer lingers, arguably out of confusion, but I sense what he is doing is saying good-bye. From a hundred yards off, I must share a measure of his sadness, this loss of his big brother. While he conducts his little wake, I pray my gratitude. It is only after he bounds away that I approach my buck. The gutting, the dragging and hanging, skinning and butchering, and, ultimately the savoring, are all to come. But for now I simply smile.

It is not this killing that feels so good. It is this living.

Diana

Artemis' counterpart in Roman mythology is Diana, goddess of the hunt and the moon. Acteon, a youthful hunter and grandson of Apollo once was caught spying on Diana, who was bathing nude in a woodland pond. His punishment for violating the sanctity of the lady's bath was to be turned into a deer. Immediately upon taking on an animal form, he was set upon by his hounds and killed.

Acteon's punishment speaks of symbolic justice as well as the values that Diana stands for. Diana is also the protectress of women. Her magic justice made Acteon become a symbol of the instinct that got him into trouble.

In art, both Artemis and Diana are often

pictured with deer, which they protect. As to their personal totems, both Greek and Roman goddesses of the hunt were most often associated with the bear, which is both an archetype of man's hunting instinct and a symbol of protection.

Saint Hubert

The eldest son of Bertrans, Duke of Aquitane, and born in 638 AD, Hubert became a prince in the House of Aquitaine in France, serving under Pepin of Heristal. Hubert enjoyed the good life of nobility, but most of all, he loved hunting. Legend has it that one Good Friday, when he should have been in church, Hubert was afield on horseback following his hounds. They cornered a large stag. As Hubert approached for the kill, suddenly a vision of a glowing crucifix appeared over the deer's head and a voice spoke: "Hubert, unless thou turnest to the Lord, and leadest a holy life, thou shalt quickly go to hell."

Hubert climbed down off his horse, begged forgiveness and asked what he should do to atone for his sins. The voice instructed him to seek guidance from Lambert, Bishop of Maastrichcht. Not long after seeking counsel with the Bishop, Hubert's wife died. He soon entered the Abbey of Staveleot, becoming a priest.

Lambert advised Hubert to make a pilgrimage to Rome in 705 AD. During Hubert's absence, Lambert was murdered. Hubert was selected by the Pope to succeed his mentor as Bishop, supposedly based on a vision. Later, Hubert built St. Peter's Cathedral in Liege, Belgium, on the spot where Lambert had died, and he in turn became the patron of the city.

Hubert applied his passion to his faith, replacing pagan rituals with Christianity in large sections of the Ardennes forest of Belgium, stretching from Meuse to the Rhine. He preached to many of the hunters of the forest, and is said to have hunted and kept dogs. Rabies was a problem for those who owned dogs, but Hubert is said to not only have been protected from the deadly disease, but to have been blessed with miraculous powers to heal rabies, aided by a special white and gold silk stole that he said was given to him by the Blessed Virgin Mary. He also had a golden key, which was reputed to be a healing amulet.

Hubert is said to have had a vision of his death, and six months later he died quietly on May 30, 727 AD, with the words "Our father, who art in heaven . . ." on his lips. In 1744, he was canonized as a saint — the patron saint of hunting and butchers.

First buried in Luttich, Hubert's body was later moved to the Andain monastary in the Ardennes, which today is known as St. Hubert's Abbey. The location of the abbey and the Belgian town of Saint Hubert is supposed to be close to where Hubert saw the stag with the cross between its antlers.

Each November 3, Saint Hubert's Day, all across France, Luxembourg, and Belgium, special masses and celebrations are held to honor Saint Hubert. During these festivities, special mass blessings are said for the safety and success of hunters and the health of their animals — dogs are blessed for protection from diseases like rabies, and special religious music written for hunting horns is performed (Grande Messe de Saint Hubert). The cumulative result of the service is to bring the spirit of the hunt right into the church and consecrate it. In certain parts of Europe, the deer hunting season is suspended to honor St. Hubert.

The physical center of devotion to Saint Hubert today remains the town of Saint Hubert in Belgium, where thousands of people, including many hunters, gather every November 3. To many European hunters, making the pilgrimage to St. Hubert on Saint Hubert's Day is like a Muslim making a pilgrimage to Mecca.

It should be noted that an almost identical story is told of the conversion of Placitus, the commander-in-chief of the Roman army of Emporer Trajan in the second century AD, who later became canonized as St. Eustace. An even earlier tale from the Middle East has a nobleman riding out on a hunt, and encountering a magical deer who transforms into a Sufi mystic, called a dervish, who admonishes the hunter to adopt a more spiritual path in life.

Celebrating St. Hubert's Day in St. Hubert, Belgium

The Festival of Saint Hubert in St. Hubert, Belgium, attracts thousands.

Every November 3, all across Europe, thousands turn out to honor Saint Hubert, patron Saint of the Hunt. The epicenter of worship is Saint Hubert's Abbey in St. Hubert, Belgium.

The Mass of Saint Hubert is celebrated with hunting horns, as hunters, dogs and falcons are invited into the church for blessings.

Hunters and hounds with the consecrated bread that is symbolic of the body of Christ.

CHAPTER 4

Animal Allies

They may be at a loss for proper words to describe a beautiful woman,
but they can eloquently describe the voices of their hounds
in words that other hunters can understand and appreciate.
The music of a pack of hounds in full cry is a spine-tingling,
heart-warming experience that lives in the hearts and
minds of these men long after the hunt is over.

—LEONARD LEE RUE III[1]

The race and point of the dogs, the well-timed flush of the grouse, and the impetuous stoop of the falcon are all essential for successful game hawking. The moments leading up to the falcon's plummeting fall through empty space mean everything to the falconer. All thoughts of the past or future vanish as the frozen pointers and hidden grouse hold time itself at bay. Falconers luxuriate in this exquisite now, unwilling to upset the delicate balance of beating hearts. They are connected through their dogs to the grouse, to the desert and the timelessness of the hunt.

CHARLES SCHWARTZ[2]

Does the mind extend beyond the body? At first thought, of course, the scientific answer is "no." Hunters are less certain. Consider the forces that bring together the hunter and the hunted. Are chance and skill all that are necessary to be at the right place at the right time? From what origins do precognitive dreams and synchronous meetings arise?

These are questions to debate long into the night, but it is obvious that the more a hunter can extend and amplify his mind and intentions, the more successful he will be. The common bond between the modern hunter and his distant ancestors is the recruitment of animal allies to expand his sphere of effectiveness. Dogs, horses and falcons are all animals that willingly aid hunters in the chase. By consent, they enable the hunter to perform special feats that the hunter alone could never accomplish, and they ask little in return, except proper care and affection. As a result, animal allies of the hunt often become some of man's closest friends.

Falcons

Using trained birds of prey — hawks, falcons, owls and eagles — as hunting allies is an ancient art. As opposed to dogs, which would have great difficulty fending for themselves if released into the wild, raptors do quite well on their own. Each time they are released, they have a choice to return or not. The bond between man and raptor thus has to be extremely strong. This extraordinary bond that keeps them together naturally lends itself to speculation about the possibilities of interspecies communication, including mental telepathy, as well as magic. Author Ursula K. Le Guin captures it best in her novel, *The Wizard of Earthsea* when she writes of the awe of the neophyte sorcerer Ged as he begins to become a falconer.

When he found that the wild falcons stooped down to him from the wind when he summoned them by name, lighting with a thunder of wings on his wrist like the hunting birds of a prince, then he hungered to know more such names and came to his aunt begging to learn the name of the sparrowhawk and the osprey and the eagle.[3]

If you wish to own a raptor, it represents a commitment. Experts recommend spending part of every day of the year with your bird, as well as providing water, space to exercise flight, shelter and lean, raw meat. Most who wish to become a falconer will study as an apprentice to a seasoned practitioner before owning his or her own bird.

Afield, each species has its own style of hunting. Harriers work best in woodlots and near cover where they can sneak up on squirrels, rabbits or roosting grouse with their silent wings. Broad-winged eagles and hawks soar to great heights before descending on prey on the ground, such as rabbits. Long-winged falcons demand the wide open spaces, where they only capture birds on the wing.

It is awe inspiring to watch a peregrine falcon descend at velocities faster than the speed of a hard-thrown fastball in order to thrust its talons into the heart of a duck that is already moving at 40 miles an hour. Such sights no doubt moved ancient naturalists to attribute godlike qualities to raptors. In Greece and Rome, the hawk was the symbol of the sun god, for it could ascend to great heights and see everything. Like so many symbolic meanings for animals, the basis is in fact, for many birds of prey have a unique quality of binocular vision, which allows them to simultaneously view the larger field of vision and zoom in for detail on one object in that field.

Some falconers use pointing dogs to locate and hold game birds. When the dog goes on point, the falcon is launched. When the raptor has reached altitude, the hunter flushes the birds into the air to witness a spectacle of spellbinding predation, as well as a remarkable event of coordination, for now three species are working together, swept into the spirit of the hunt.

Then there are those who ride horses to keep up with their dogs and falcons. Each new ally lends more power to the quest, as well as a higher level of challenge to keep them working together.

Horses

At first, horses were game. In 1995, at an open-pit coal mine at Shoeningen, 60 miles east of Hanover, Germany, archeologist Hartmut Thieme of the Institut fuer Denkmalpflege retrieved a cache of stone and wooden tools and bones from the path of a developer's bulldozer. Carbon dating of several six- to seven-foot-long wooden spears found beside piles of animal bones, mostly horses, has placed the artifacts at 400,000 years old. Writing in the science journal *Nature*, Thieme says that he believes Homo erectus, predecessor to our present species, Homo sapiens, would have

Fox Hunting on Horseback

> . . . *what a good huntsman should be: he should be young, strong active, bold and enterprising; fond of diversions and indefatigable in the pursuit of it; he should be sensible and good-tempered; he also ought to be sober; he should be exact, civil and cleanly; he should be a good horseman and a good groom; his voice should be strong and clear; and he should have an eye so quick, as to perceive which of his hounds carries the scent when all are running; and he should have so excellent an ear, always to distinguish the foremost hounds when he does not see them; he should be quiet, patient and without conceit.*

PETER BECKFORD[4]

used the spears. This find and his conclusion suggest that the instinct to hunt was passed along from other species.

Among the animals that we use for transporting us — horses, elephants, camels, and burros — the horse is the speediest. Just carrying our gear makes horses indispensable in rugged country, but they have agreed to carry us as well. Horses add speed, strength, endurance, and jumping ability to our frame, enabling pursuit that would otherwise be impossible. How long man has been riding horses is not clear. It most likely began with the capture of a young animal that was tamed and trained. What an enormous breakthrough that must have been!

Dogs

All members of the canine family are carnivorous hunters. Domestication in itself is a radical change in behavior. The fact that some species have learned to continue the chase, but not devour the game killed by the hunter, is a remarkable achievement in evolution and trust.

Dogs have been hunters' allies for at least 10,000 years, while some suggest 150,000. Bred from wild canines to enhance certain traits, each breed has special attributes — pointers, setters, retrievers, flushers, trackers, etc. One remarkable dog is the gray or black Scandinavian dog that looks like a miniature husky, commonly called an elk hound, that carries its tail curled on its back. In reality the dog is not a hound nor does it hunt elk, but it surely is among the most skilled of all hunting allies. The Norwegian elghund (proper spelling) is a member of the spitz group, a breed that is at least 8,000 years-old. While they make lovable pets, the dogs imprint heavily on one person. In the days of the Vikings, elghunds were buried with ship captains so that they would be able to continue the hunt in Valhalla.

Elghunds can hunt small game, but they are especially skilled at tracking and holding large game, such as moose. They trail by following airborne scent, and when a moose is cornered, they hold it at bay for upwards of an hour and a half while barking shrilly to let the hunters know where the moose is. Some elghunds are also specially trained to track wounded game, following blood trails much like bloodhounds. Some antihunters argue that using dogs is cruel and inhumane. First, from the dog's perspective, it would be inhumane to deny them the opportunity to hunt, for it's in their nature. Second, a dog that holds game for the hunter makes it easier for the hunter to make a killing, humane shot, and to track down wounded animals.

There is an extraordinary bond between a man and his hunting dog, which sometimes takes on almost supernatural qualities, as Dr. Michael Billig of Vermont, a passionate duck hunter and conservationist, relates in the following story.

Dr. Michael Billig

I have a passion for all hunting, but for me, the last few days of the duck season are profound, maybe even a religious experience. That's when I go hunting eider ducks on the Maine coast.

You always go out to hunt eiders with a lump in your throat. It's bitter, icy cold, often snowing, and dangerous. You are dealing with a nine-and-a-half-foot tide, then maybe four to five-foot swells on top of that. I have had three friends die from drowning while hunting ducks. It's part of the bargain you strike with nature: you risk your neck in

exchange for one of the most exhilarating experiences you can have with nature.

Once you've laid out your decoys and gotten set up in the rocks, these large, elegant black-and-white birds start coming. Common eiders. Really noble birds. Big, stunning, elegant, beautiful. I have a pair mounted in my study that reminds me of them every day.

If you shoot an eider, retrieving it can be quite a chore. Sometimes downright life threatening if you have to use a boat. A good dog is essential. I like Chesapeake Bay retrievers. One of my most memorable days out eider hunting I can recall is a time when we went out early in the morning after an ice storm. The ocean was swarming with phosphorescence. Every dip of the paddle in the water would leave what looked like a shower of sparks on the surface. We took a longer route to get to the blind just to watch the iridescent colors shooting out all around the boat. When the dog would hit the water, he would send up a spray like a thousand fireflies were swarming around him.

I had one Chessie for nearly 11 years. His name was Burt, and he was all heart. When he finally died, I felt lost. A few months later, we went to visit a friend who had a Chessie with a new litter of puppies. They were three to four weeks old. My wife sat down beside the whelping box. One of them crawled out of the box and came over to play with my wife. He chose us, and the relationship soon became mutual. We named him Isaac, which means laughter. He was filled with energy, lovable and smart. We took him home when he was eight weeks old. In two or three months he was retrieving. A really smart, lovable dog. He was easily trained to not go into the road by the house, but one day when he was a little less than a year old, he strayed out into the road playing with another dog. Isaac got hit by a car and was killed. We were devastated.

My son was living in England at the time. A friend of ours, who is a dowser, and maybe a psychic, told us that Isaac's soul would be reborn in a dog in England. She said that I would know which one he was because if I looked him in the face he would return my gaze. Not long after that, my son called to tell us about a litter of Chesapeake Bay retrievers that was to be born to a dog in Wales. It felt right, so my wife and I got plane tickets to see my son, as well as to check out the dogs.

The dogs were about eight weeks old when we arrived. We walked into the kennel. There were two males in the litter that I felt drawn to. I picked up one. He wouldn't return my stare. I put him down. When I picked up the other one he immediately looked me right in the eye as if he knew me.

We took the two males out in the field to watch them play. They were both healthy. Then an idea came to me. I'm a chiropractor, and part of the diagnostic process I perform on patients is to test the strengths and weaknesses of various muscles. It's called applied kineseology. I've found that it not only is an accurate measure of the organic health of the body, but it can shed light on emotional and mental issues as well, picking up things you might not be conscious of. Well, I took the two dogs and picked them up individually and asked my son to muscle test me when I held each dog. When I held the one male, who would not look me in the eye, I was weaker. When I held the one that had returned me gaze, I was stronger.

The woman who owned the litter seemed a little unnerved. I tried to explain about applied kineseology as a diagnostic tool. I ended my explanation jokingly with the remark that some people called me a witch doctor. Then she was even more rattled. She took me back to see the pedigree papers for my new dog. Now I was flabbergasted. His official name, which was selected before I arrived, was Pennrose of Witch Doctor.

When we were finished drawing up the papers, I went back to the barn. I walked inside and called out to the whelping box, "Alright Isaac, let's go home." The dog I had selected (maybe I should say we selected each other) left the litter and with God as my witness, he came running right over to me. The only dog who moved when I called. Eight weeks old and he had not seen me more than two hours. At that point my son could only shake his head.

The new Isaac has been a wonderful dog. He has proven to be a magnificent male with a wonderful disposition. A real natural birder. A dog like Isaac is not just an animal that performs a task on my call. We're really a team, connected on more levels than I can fathom, or maybe even care to admit.

CHAPTER

Magical Skills

The hunter must not only know about the habits of his prey,
he also must know that there are powers on this earth that guide
men and animals and everything that is living.

—CARLOS CASTANEDA[1]

Shrinking the distance between the hunter and the hunted is a chief preoccupation of hunters. The closer one gets to the animal the greater the chance of making a killing shot. Modern firearms extend the lethal striking powers of the hunter, but as weaponry becomes more sophisticated, so too become the animals. Many hunters will attest to the fact that the hunted seem to quickly come to an understanding of the safe distance to man. Modern deer are especially good at this. On more than one occasion, I have seen feeding deer walk into a field where shooters were shooting skeet and trap. As if oblivious to the loud shots ringing out, the deer would approach to 150 yards or so and feed, showing no signs of any fear, even when tiny shot would rain down around them. In another time or place, to approach such deer with 300 yards might be considered skillful.

Calls

Successfully mimicking a wild animal, one ultimately joins with the clan of that species. Outdoor writer Jim Casada shares the secrets of calling wild turkeys with a call made from the wingbone of the birds.

The Wingbone Call

The origins of the wingbone reach back into the dark, mysterious recesses of the past. One would like to think that the discovery of the wingbone's efficacy went something like this: A small party of hunters, after an arduous day's quest, manages to kill two or three turkeys near sunset. Famished, they hastily build a fire and cook the birds. As the feast progresses, one of the hunters, anxious to obtain every bit of succulent goodness from the turkeys, gnaws the end of a wingbone off to suck out the tasty, nutritious marrow. As he inhales, the unmistakable sound of a turkey's cluck suddenly fills the air. When he recovers from shock, he repeats the suction and soon discovers how to yelp like a turkey with the aid of the bird's own bones.

Native Americans also used leaves from plants including yellow jasmine and green brier to make turkey sounds. Small sections of river cane and elderberry (both of which have pith that can easily be extracted to make a hollow tube) also were fashioned into calls. But, for a Native American closely rooted in the earth and spiritually connected to his prey, the ability to elicit the sounds to call in other birds would surely have held special meaning.

At some point in time, countless generations later, observant European settlers discovered the Indian's knack for drawing turkeys into close range with a wingbone call. They borrowed the tool and turned it into a devastating tool of slaughter. Many of the market hunters who supplied wild turkeys to the eager palates of city dwellers of the 19th century used a wingbone call. In time, as most students of modern wildlife conservation readily realize, the wild turkey's numbers plunged dramatically.

This was, of course, no fault of the wingbone, but rather those who misused it and abused the good earth and her resources. The comeback of the wild turkey, from a total U.S. wild flock of around 30,000 right after the Great Depression, to more than 4 million today is one of the great conservation sagas of the 20th century.

There are many ways to coax His Majesty, the wild turkey, into range, but no calling

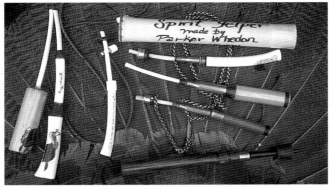

notes thrill the human ear as they filter alluringly through the greening up woods of spring.

Most of all, the wingbone's spiritual link with turkeys from bygone hunts holds the hunter's soul in thrall. Each time I take to the woods — with a call fashioned from wingbones taken from the first hen and first gobbler I ever killed hanging from my neck — it is with the knowledge that it adorns me as a true totem. The call is a visible connection which, through the magic of sound, allows me to communicate with my prey. The wingbone holds me in bondage as its sounds seduce turkeys, and to experience the symbolic link is to understand why the wingbone is truly wondrous.

device matches the wingbone. It is difficult to master, and not for everyone, yet the effort required to learn its use, history and origins sets the call apart. So does, in greater degree, its mystique. It calls those who have come under its spell as surely as its dulcet note calls turkeys. Its soft patina, the product of long, loving years of use, draws the eye like the polished glossiness of old ivory; its sure sweet

Making Your Own Wingbone Call

For those who prefer an almost spiritual sense of connection with their prey, fashioning a wingbone yelper is a fairly simple undertaking. Patience, a quality that looms large in all hunting, is required, as are a few simple tools. Perhaps the most difficult part of the process is obtaining the requisite raw materials, because to make a wingbone call that sounds like a hen, you need the mouthpiece portion of the call to come from the radial bone of a hen. This is the smaller of the two bones in the middle joint of the wing. Use of a jake's (young male) radius produces the sounds of an adolescent gobbler, while that of a mature tom emits the coarse, raspy notes made by a grown gobbler. In each instance, it is best to fashion the bell or trumpet end of the call from the ulna or humerus of a gobbler.

When properly used, this type of call works

wondrously well. It nicely reproduces clucks, yelps and cutts. In the hands of a truly proficient caller, wingbones can also be used to kee-kee and even gobble. Mastering the complete range takes considerable practice, but the rewards make the effort worthwhile.

Wingbone calls come in several forms, but to my way of thinking as I suggested above, the simplest one — utilizing two bones — is the most effective. Once you have obtained the bones — and this may be from turkeys you have killed, those taken by friends, road kills or the like — you are ready to get down to business. Incidentally, do not despair about obtaining hen wingbones. There are a number of states where either-sex fall hunting is allowed, and you might spread the word to local wildlife officers that you would appreciate a radial bone or two from any road, predator, or

poacher killed ones they might find.

Begin by boiling the bones in water for a quarter to half an hour. Then use a dull pocketknife or sandpaper to remove remaining bits of flesh and cartilage. Once the bones are clean, use a jigsaw or rat-tail file to cut away the joints. Cut as close to the end as possible. This will leave a slightly flattened area for the mouthpiece and a flare on the trumpet end of the call. Remove the marrow from inside the bones with a wire or pipe cleaner.

With the cleaned and dried bones, begin to assemble the yelper. Insert the more rounded end of the radial bone (the opposite, flatter end will be the mouthpiece) a quarter inch into the small end of the gobbler ulna, positioning the two bones so that the call makes a gentle curve or arc. With the bones properly aligned, bond them with heavy-duty glue, making sure that no glue enters the air passage. Wrap the joint with tape or thread for added strength and air tightness. Push a pipe cleaner through the joint to make certain there is no residue of glue in the passage. After the glue has dried, add the finishing touches. A piece cut from a rubber bottle stopper with a hole in the middle can be fitted over the mouthpiece for use as a mouth stop. Adjust it to allow the call to fit properly over your lips. If desired, a lanyard can be attached where the two bones join. Some artists even paint or scrimshaw the trumpet end as a final touch.

Running a wingbone call properly takes considerable practice, and it is something better taught through actions than with words. For present purposes, suffice it to say that you obtain sound by sucking or smacking in a kissing-like fashion while pulling air from deep within your throat. Both hands are used to cup the trumpet end of the call and create an adjustable sound chamber. Clucks are the easiest call to learn, and they are produced by a sharp, quick intake of breath in a sucking fashion. Next progress to yelps, striving to get the clear "kee-owk" break in sound as you do so. The wingbone call does this better than any type of calling device. Cutting is nothing more than a fast-paced series of clucks, and perhaps you can then move on to other turkey sounds. In every instance, the adage "practice makes perfect" is applicable.

The Legend of Gluskap, Creator of the Moose Call

Among the Indians of northeastern North America, principally the Abenaki, Penobscot, and Micmac, there is a tale that the birch bark megaphone used to call moose was first invented by the legendary hero Gluskap (sometimes Glooscap). The story goes that, a long time ago, the Indians were terrorized by a giant, bloodthirsty moose who would raid vil-

"Calling A Moose" photograph by Edward Curtis

lages and trample all who could not escape his giant hooves and antlers. In desperation, the people prayed to the Great Spirit, Gitche Manitou, who heard their pleas and sent the hero, Gluskap, whose name, incidentally, also means Liar, for Gluskap is a master weaver of stories.

Gluskap set out to find the horrible moose. He met many terrified people whose homes had been smashed by the giant moose, but Gluskap could not track down the killer moose. Finally, Gluskap retreated to a dense grove of sacred spruce trees where he prayed and fasted, asking for guidance from Gitche Manitou about how to stop the destruction. Ultimately, he received guidance in visions and voices on the wind.

When Gluskap came back to the people, he chose four young men and instructed them to go and cut strips of white birch bark from living trees, but to not harm the trees. When they brought him the bark, he began to build a megaphone, lacing it together with the roots of a spruce tree. The length was a man's forearm. At the large end it was the diameter of a hand. The small end was the width of two fingers.

With this medicine horn, Gluskap strode to the edge of the forest and began to grunt and whine, imitating the call of the lovesick cow moose. In the distance, a crashing of trees came thundering back as the giant bull announced to all that he would fight to the death for the love of this cow. Gluskap called some more, changing his tone to be ever so seductive. Soon, the giant moose came striding out of the forest, leaving a swath of broken trees behind.

The people of the village shrank back in terror. Gluskap, however, stood his ground. As the moose approached him, Gluskap extended his arm upward, and it kept going and going until it reached the back of the moose. The moose froze in his tracks and could not flee. Gluskap then began to push downward, shrinking the size of the moose until it was about the size of a large horse. Then, he took his hand away.

Gluskap addressed the moose, shaming him for the death and destruction he had caused. He said that because he had caused the people so much misery and hardship, Gitche Manitou was angry. Henceforth, forever after, the moose would remain about the size of a horse, and each fall when the moon of falling leaves came, the Indian people would be able to use this call to bring the moose out of the forest so some could be killed for food.[2]

Decoys

Ducks and geese prefer crowds. Decoys are an essential part of a waterfowl hunter's equipment. They serve as representations placed on land or water, designed to convince birds that a waterfowl meeting is underway and, thus, attract them into shooting range. Native hunters made decoys out of clumps of mud and sticks, birch bark, woven tule and cedar branches. Often, they would skin ducks and geese, and pull the skins over the rough forms to make extraordinarily effective decoys.

Fresh birds just down from the north will sometimes readily flock into sets of plastic cleanser jugs, bottles, and cans painted appropriate colors. That naiveté doesn't last long. Soon, birds become very wary and carefully assess a decoy spread with the eyes of a hawk. Especially on large bodies of water, a hunter may need 100 decoys or more to pull in birds from a distance. Before the days of plastic, this many decoys would represent a sizable investment, so many people in the good old days made their own.

For many years, most decoys were made from wood, the body carved from the lightest wood available, and the heads made from pine or fir to be more durable. In southern Michigan, the preferred wood for making decoy bodies was cedar, and the best source was old, weathered utility poles. New poles were soaked

A BRIEF EVOLUTIONARY HISTORY OF DECOYS FROM
THE INDIAN WOVEN-CEDAR DECOY TO THE
WOODEN DECOY TO THE MODERN PLASTIC AND
PHOTOGRAHIC SILHOUETTE. WHAT THE OLDER
DECOYS LACKED IN MIMICRY, THEY BALANCED WITH
SOUL.

in creosote, which fouled tools and was a health hazard. The black, oily substance was well leached out of the old poles, though, and the best time to get this prized wood was in the dead of winter when an ice storm came along and the poles were pulled down by the weight of the ice-covered lines. As soon as the roads were passable, the old-timers would rush out to cut the sweet-smelling cedar poles into 15- to 17-inch sections. Back home, they'd split them in two with an ax or splitting mall, yielding two body blocks per section. With a hatchet, they'd whittle down the block some more, and then put it into a big vice, where the tool of choice to bring it into shape was a spoke shave, or draw knife, followed by a wood rasp and some sandpaper for the finishing touches.

Used 2 x 4s make respectable heads. Cut them on a jigsaw — long sloping heads for canvasbacks, high foreheads for scaup and redheads, and chunky lines for mallards. Drill head and body with a three-eighths-inch bit and then join the two with a wooden dowel. Until epoxy came along, Weldwood glue was used to hold them together. Paint was flat enamel. Scaup, or bluebills, were the easiest to decorate, as the males are black and white with a bluish-gray bill and a yellow eye.

Art is always a partial projection of the interior landscape of the artist, as well as the subject of the work. In the old wooden decoys that were so popular until the 1950s when cork, Styrofoam, fiberglass and plastic decoys began to come on the market, you could always see a

hint of the soul of the old duck hunters. Those decoys were not always perfect representations of the birds, but they had a raw, primal quality that made them seem to come alive in the water. Those decoys had an ability to pull in ducks like nothing else I've ever hunted with.

When I was young, I learned to carve from some old market hunters. They took me hunting, too. In contrast to some modern sport hunters who shoot at passing birds on the wing, the old-timers I hunted with had the patience of saints. They would wait as the ducks circled the decoys, sometimes four or five times, and then landed. Then, they would shoot at the birds sitting on the water.

At first, I protested this practice. It wasn't sporting, I argued. They responded, asking if I intended to eat the ducks or not. Of course I did, I replied. "Well, if you shoot a duck on the water, all you hit is its head and back, and you don't eat them parts," one old-timer explained. "You shoot 'em in the air, when they are landing, and you tear up the breast, fill it with lead. Ruins the meat if you're too good a shot."

Clothing

Hunting is only partially about eating.
The other part . . . is about the gods.

DUDLEY YOUNG[1]

Aside from practical matters such as keeping one warm and dry, a hunter's clothes have at least two primary but opposite functions — concealment, enabling them to get closer to their prey, or announcement, signaling the hunter's presence as boldly as possible for safety reasons. There are, however, other considerations in choosing a hunter's wardrobe.

While few hunters would deny the existence of beginner's luck, success at hunting often calls upon all the tools and skills available. Clothing, jewelry and costumes of hunters often include elements associated with wishes for good fortune. The hat, coat or gun of an admired hunter carries positive associations: memories, their feel or style. A brand of bow or boot suggested by an acknowledged expert reminds one of their skills as well as their knowledge.

Objects and decorations linked with a desire to influence events may use a variety of methods to attract powers. Technically speaking, an amulet is an article of wood, stone, metal or bone upon which symbols and designs have been inscribed. Through sympathetic magic, these markings are believed to attract good fortune or ward off evil. Amulets take on extra power when they have been handed down from revered hunters who have passed on.

A talisman has inscriptions of mythical beings, such as signs of the zodiac, and has been consecrated in a ritual to imbue it with magical powers. A common practice among

"STAG HUNTING" BY THEODORE DE BRY IS A HAND-COLORED ETCHING OF A 1564 ACCOUNT OF THE TIMACULA INDIANS OF FLORIDA HUNTING DEER WITH DEERSKIN COSTUMES FOR CONCEALMENT.

THE SACRED ART OF HUNTING

KWAKIUTL CHIEF SIWIDI

native hunters is to mark their hunting weapons with a dab of their own urine, much the way an animal might mark its territory.

Charms, such as a rabbit's foot, are associated with bringing good luck, based on legends and folk beliefs that trace back many years. The origin of the rabbit's foot as a good luck charm, for example, is said to be derived from the ability of rabbits to avoid predators by speed and agility.

Cresting arrows, for example, adds beauty, helps locate them, and identifies the shooter. However, an arrow becomes an amulet when its crest design originates from a dream or a vision, identifies membership in a society of hunters, or is prescribed by a shaman.

ABOVE: THREE HUNTING AMULETS:
The good luck hunting amulets displayed on this skin come from three different native traditions. The circular bracelet is African, a tracker charm originating from the bushmen of Zambia. It is made from the tail hair of an elephant. It cannot be bought; it must be given by its maker as a wish of good luck and admiration. This bracelet is from the late noted African hunter Peter Hathaway Capstick. The necklace is Saami from Scandinavia. The leather is reindeer hide and the metal pendant is the symbol of a shaman, or noajadie, who is the intermediary between man, the animals and the spirit world. The bear claw, worn on clothing or as a pendant, is seen worldwide as a hunter's charm. The bear is the animal most like man, and he is an excellent hunter. Frequently, in native cosmologies, the bear is the one animal that can communicate with all others.

RIGHT: MODERN HUNTER'S CLOSET:
The search for that perfect camouflage has become a multi-million dollar fashion industry.

. . . the characteristics of a bird or an animal were desired by the Indians who, in some cases, wore a part of the bird or animal on their persons; the deer, because the animal can endure thirst a long time; the hawk as the surest bird of prey, the elk in gallantry; the frog in watchfulness; the owl in night-wisdom and gentle ways; the bear, which though fierce, has given many medicinal herbs for the good of man; the kit-fox, which is active and wily; the crow, which is especially direct as well as swift in flight; and the wolf, in hardihood.

FRANCES DENSMORE[2]

Weapons

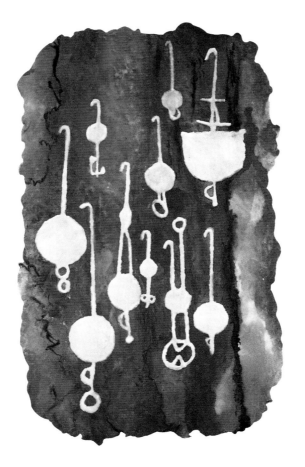

*And when everything clicks, it is as if the shotgun were a set of talons
or jaws or a beak, a potent extension of the body — one points with
the left hand, out in front, gripping the barrels, the shot is loosed,
it reaches out from the brain and the soul, through wood and metal,
through thin air, to intercept the wild fleeting form.*

CHARLES FERGUS[1]

The first hunters relied more on entrapment than marksmanship with a weapon. Snares, traps, and deadfalls to catch animals — or in the case of large herd animals like buffalo, stampeding them over a cliff — were all very effective and safe techniques that conserved time and energy. Weapons, which came later, are a physical extension of man's intention, translated into technology. Prior to their invention, only the chimpanzee, who uses sticks, used weapons. (Chimpanzees incidentally, also engage in sport hunting.)

A weapon, on one hand, is a material object designed with lethal intention. Precision, utility and accuracy are factored in with a blend of science and art. On the other hand, it is a close friend, a benefactor, and maybe even a protector that saves your life. Every hunter remembers his first gun as much as his first kiss. When you acquire a weapon that fits you like a glove, often it gets a name, like Daniel Boone's rifle Old Betsy, or Davy Crockett's Lucretia Borgia. To many, weapons have souls.

In earlier times, weapons-making was a magical art, filled with secrets and charged with ritual. Eskimos sought to impart a soul, *inua*, into their weapons with carvings and rituals, so that the weapon would guide itself to the mark. On many wooden weapons (spears, arrows and atlatls) one finds carvings of either a hunter's totem — such as a snake, an eagle or a bear — or the intended prey. In the latter case one would assume that the hunter hoped to use sympathetic magic to draw his weapon and his prey together.

The power of a weapon is dependent upon how far its projectile can be accurately cast at a target, and its ability to inflict mortal wounds. Tracing the evolution of a weapon sheds light on its unique spirit.

Guns

The forerunner of the bullet was a thrown rock. Its potency grew when a stone-throwing sling allowed the hunter to cast the rock farther and with more accuracy and ease. Tying the rocks to strings created a flying spider web to entangle the wings and feet of birds. Some early hunting bows cast rocks from a pouch like a modern slingshot. These were lethal for small game and birds.

Krieghoff's engraved Diana shotgun

The stone took on more power when man discovered how to harness fire to create a confined explosion. Ingenuity replaced muscle power when the driving force became a chemical reaction. Marksmanship took a giant step forward.

Gunpowder — a mixture of potassium nitrate, charcoal and sulfur — originated in China over 1,000 years ago as a propellant for fireworks. A German monk, Bertold Schwarz, is believed to be the first person to use gunpowder as a propellant for projectiles. It was the first explosive, and by the mid-1300s there were gunpowder factories throughout Europe. Even today, in Chinese factories where gunpowder is used or manufactured, people work in silence. It is said that talking or making excessive noise dishonors the spirit of gunpowder.

Guns and bullets are made from metal. The gunsmith who makes them, is then a blacksmith. Quality of craftsmanship has an influence on weaponry, but once the blacksmith was seen as a wizard, whose alchemical symbol is the salamander—a species known for its dramatic transformation from aquatic to terrestrial existence. Metals once were cast based on secret formulas that blended ingredients (hair of animals, traces of rare elements, blessed materials, etc.), incantations, ritual procedures and spoken spells into the practical craft of metal-making. The resulting weapons became magical implements with personalities, aided by guiding spirits.

Both metal and wooden parts of guns can be engraved with a myriad of symbols. Some call to mind memories of days afield or the animals sought. Others make artistic statements of faith or perform invocations of spiritual forces that the hunter hopes will improve his chances of hitting the quarry and killing it quickly and cleanly.

Archery

Some Australian aborigines . . . say that the bow and arrow came into existence when the bow ancestor and his string wife — who is always embracing him, having her arms around his neck — came to earth and revealed to mankind how to construct a bow and arrow and then disappeared again. . .

MARIE-LOUISE VON FRANZ[2]

The sharpened stone became a knife, the sharp edges killing by hemorrhaging. Binding it to a wooden shaft, the knife became a spear, extending the range of the hunter, as well as affording more safe distance between the hunter and dangerous animals. Creating a device to extend the leverage of the spearthrower, and making a lighter projectile resulted in an atlatl capable of casting a shaft in excess of 50 yards. Imagine the Paleolithic genius who first discovered how attaching a string to a bent stick resulted in a device that could cast a light, lethal spear — now called an arrow — over 100 yards. That technological breakthrough remains one of the most profound in human history. It revolutionized hunting and warfare, and gave us a popular recreational activity enjoyed by millions all around the world.

For Pastor Brent Rudolph, making archery tackle has become a path to making friendships that bridge wide rivers of faith:

Bow hunting has always been part of my life, as has church. Being raised in a small Baptist church by devout Christian parents made it easy for me to find faith in God. My relationship with God grew and as a young man I received a calling from the Lord to the ministry. I serve as a pastor now, and during my sermons in my humble Montana congregation I see the same far away look in the eyes of a few of the youth that I had as a boy, thinking of bucks when everyone else was listening to the service.

My love for archery led me to learn the art

of bow building. This process has provided me with the opportunity to make some life-long relationships that I will always treasure. Ron Hardcastle has been one of those treasures. "Why not build a Turkish style bow of modern components?" he asked me one night over coffee at a restaurant. He handed me a copy of Dr. Paul Klopsteg's book, *Turkish Archery and The Composite Bow.* I flipped through the pages thinking that this is the most strikingly beautiful bow that I had ever seen. I had always been a fan of short bows, but this wasn't just a short bow, it was a won-

der. After a few cups of java, we had a blue-print drawn out on no less than a napkin. The Sultan was born, and my passion for Turkish archery has flourished since that day. I find it a very honorable form of archery, full of history and tradition.

I have gained so much from the development of this bow. One gentleman with a physical handicap from a shoulder injury was told he would have to stop shooting archery, or would have to learn to shoot a compound bow. This short bow has turned out to work just fine for him.

Another gentleman who has a wealth of information and reference material deepened my interest in the art of eastern archery by sharing its tie to the Islamic faith. Being a man of the cloth, this excited me to no end. We spent hours discussing the spiritual aspects of the sport and sharing our faiths with each other. We found that we both serve a God, and we both were avid archers. The two seem totally disconnected from each other by some, yet we found something of a common thread in the bow that allowed us to discuss spiritual matters in depth. I am still Christian and Mahoud is still Islamic, but we are both archers. Throughout history men have killed each other in the name of religion, but for a brief moment in time, two men of seemingly radically different opposing views of faith were shooting with each other instead of at each other.

Building an eastern-flavored bow has given me a chance to speak with other Islamic shooters. I also find them passionate and dedicated to the sport, perhaps as Sir Robert Ainsle did some 200 years ago. In all, these relationships have broadened me and made me a better person. God as well as the bow are able to cross over cultural and social barriers to bring people together on a common ground.

God bless our world leaders that they would find the same pleasures in life as good friends and a good bow. "I take away the chariots from Ephram and the war-horses from Jerusalem, and the battle bow will be broken. He will proclaim peace to the nations. His rule will extend from sea to sea and from the River to the ends of the earth" (Zec 9:10 NIV).

Marksmanship

Practice, practice, practice, practice and more practice until shooting becomes automatic and true. D.T. Suzuki once said of mastering the art of shooting a bow and arrow: "If one really wishes to be a master of an art, technical knowledge of it is not enough. One has to transcend technique so that the art becomes an 'artless art' growing out of the unconscious."[3]

When this state is attained, Suzuki maintained the hunter no longer consciously makes the shot. Rather, it seems as though the bow shoots itself the way that snow slips off a branch.

Wingshooters perfect their skills by shooting clay pigeons thrown by a slingshot device, which is called skeet shooting. "Skeet" is a Scandinavian word for "shooting."

Actor Robert Stack was U.S. National Skeet Shooting Champion at age 17 and is enshrined in the Skeet Shooting Hall of Fame. How to improve your marksmanship? Aside from practice, practice and more practice, Stack offers the following advice on how to be a better shot:

If you have never tried skeet shooting, imagine what it would be like to hit a moving object with a stream of water from a garden hose. It's not enough to aim directly for the object, because there's a split-second delay between your shot and the moment you hit the moving target. So you have to shoot where your instincts tell you the target will be.

ROBERT STACK[4]

The Hunting Grounds

*Hunting in my experience — and by hunting I simply mean being out
on the land — is a state of mind. All of one's faculties are brought to
bear in an effort to become fully incorporated into the landscape.
. . . To hunt means to have the land around you like clothing.*

—Barry Lopez[1]

In western Nevada, half an hour south of Reno as the crow flies, lies an archeological site called Grimes Point. On close inspection, the suitcase-sized dark rocks are covered with petroglyphs that look like snakes. Grimes Point is thought to be a hunting increase site, where Shoshonean Indians once performed ceremonies associated with driven hunts for jackrabbits, antelope, deer and sage grouse. There are other rocky places nearby. Why this place? Chance? I doubt it. D. H. Lawrence once wrote of the power of place:

> Every continent has its own great spirit of place. Every people is polarized in some particular locality, which is home, the homeland. Different places on the face of the earth have different vital effluence, different vibration, different chemical exhalation, different polarity with different stars: call it what you like but the spirit of place is a great reality.[2]

The Japanese have a tradition that the spirits of certain animals are associated with certain special places, *reiteki*. Each place has a different presiding spirit, *kami*. Mount Wakakusa, near Nara on the main island of Honshu in Japan, is associated with the deer

spirit. Each year on January 15, Shinto priests set fire to vegetation on the mountain. This is to ensure that the herd of roughly 1,000 deer in Nara-Koen Park will have ample food for the year. These deer are said to be descendants of a white deer who in ancient times transported on its back a wise old man so he could deliver a very important message to the emperor. To commemorate the sacred deer of Nara at the Kasuga Tashi shrine on Mount Wakakusa, more than 2,000 concrete lanterns, each bearing the symbol of a deer, are lit every February 2 or 3 and August 15.

Seeking game, a hunter cultivates a feel for the land that goes beyond the five senses. Yes, appropriate habitat — the right blend of food, water, shelter — is essential for each species. You need to know the right kind of habitat for the species you hunt. But there are those special places that draw animals like magnets for no apparent reason. Often these places seem to have a subtle feeling of richness about them. It is hard to put into words, but there is a very slight feeling of extra life there. Animals know what I'm talking about. When a hunter finds such places, they become prized secrets. When one has access to such a place, they understand why *Valhalla* of Scandinavia mythology and the American Indian *happy hunting ground* are both equated with heaven. What every hunter dreams of is to find a piece of heaven on earth.

We mark prized hunting grounds with fences and signs to restrict access as well as delineate our piece of paradise. A Mongolian hunting outfitter once told me that among certain tribes in his native land, hunters embarking on the hunt traditionally pass under a tripod of 12- to 15-foot-long wooden stakes that are laced together into a teepee-like form. Each stave of the three is decorated with

ONE OF 2,000 LANTERNS HONORING THE DEER AT NARA-KOEN PARK IN JAPAN.

Life-size 9,000 year-old
reindeer petroglyph in
Boularein, Sweden, marking a
hunting ground

brightly colored ribbons that
wave gaily in the wind. The
ribbons are similar in purpose to wishes and prayers
written on paper that one
finds attached to tree
branches at outdoor shrines
in Japan — appeals to the
gods for guidance, support
and protection. The symbol-
ism of the tripod was that of a portal or
entrance into another world that the hunter
enters when taking afield: the world of the
hunt. Upon returning from hunting, the
hunter is supposed to pass under the same tripod, signifying that he is leaving the mindset
of the hunter behind and returning to regular
cultural norms.

There is also a human element that is factored into the spirit of a place. The Chinese
geomancers or Feng Shui speak of the predecessor factor of a place: what has taken place
there before. They believe that place has a
memory. If good things and people have previously used a place, they leave behind a
subtle beneficial change in the spirit of a
place. One may scoff at such things, but
using a stand or a blind once occupied by
special people has appeal.

Hunters hold deep reverence for certain
hunting places. They become like family
members. Just speaking their names is like
uttering a blessing. Scott Stouder, editor of
Mule Deer magazine, shares a story about a
special Oregon ridge where several generations of his family have taken their first deer
or elk.

Middle Ridge

BY SCOTT STOUDER

Names connect us with places. Places like
Deep Creek, The Rocky Draw and The
Long Ridge could be anywhere. But to those
who have hunted, climbed and camped in the
canyons and contours of each namesake, each
has a special meaning — a personal connection.

Middle Ridge, a heavily timbered divide
ridge between two forks of an Oregon coastal
stream, was just a name I'd heard my relatives
talk about when I was growing up. It was a
special place to my family before I was born.
In 1936 my grandfather stood beside my
father as he killed his first elk on the ridge. In
the 1950's my mother killed her first elk near
the horse trail that later became a logging
road. But it became a special place to me
when I killed my first elk there when I was 14
years old. The place — Middle Ridge — initiated me into the hunt and became my
teacher in my younger years. Later, much
of its magic was destroyed by logging and
roads, but those early experiences would

guide my relationship with other places I would hunt and the animals that I hunted.

The summer my daughter, Susan, turned twelve years old she passed a hunter education class. This girl, who collected American Girl dolls, sang in the Heart of The Valley Choir and was on the volleyball and basketball teams, said she wanted to hunt. When her nonhunting friends asked her how she could kill an animal, she answered truthfully that she didn't know if she could.

That fall we hunted a section of Middle Ridge that had escaped the bulldozers and chain saws. On a stormy November day we searched the alder benches and evergreen jungles for a deer. Suddenly, in the wet-world of a Pacific Coast rain storm, a three-point buck emerged, meeting our stare with his own.

"Can you see him?" I whispered.

"I can see him," she said, her voice creeping toward frustration. "But the crosshairs are bouncing all over the place." The previous summer we'd shot paper targets together, but this was the first time she'd ever held a rifle with the intent to kill. The young deer and girl faced each other through 75 yards of driving rain under the canopy of 140-year-old fir trees and centuries of evolution. I watched the ageless scene with the will of a hunter and the heart of a father, but I was only a spectator.

"I can't shoot standing up," she said finally, as the buck continued to stand motionless. Deliberately she sat down in the leaf-littered salal brush, rested the rifle on her knee, snuggled up to the scope and touched the trigger.

The crack of the rifle was lost to the wind and rain.

"Did I get him?" she asked, letting out ragged breaths after the shot.

"Yes," I said. "You got him."

As I watched my daughter run to where the buck lay, I thought of this place and how much it — and hunting — has meant to my life.

I hunt because I was raised to hunt.

The torch of hunting was passed to me by my father as it was passed to him by his father.

The beauty of a elk bugle in the cold mountain air, the excitement of a fresh track, the joy of walking quietly, the pride of a clean kill — those are my family's values that live through me. They are as deeply etched in my soul as the memories they invoke.

The reasons I hunt are firmly embedded in family and tradition. But, as valuable as those reasons are — and as dear the memories — they are not the full reasons I hunt.

I hunt for the joy of hunting. But if I could not connect that joy to consumption, the roots of my life would be tenuous. I hunt, and kill, for the meat. I do not shy, nor will I shield myself from the conscious act of killing by allowing others to do it for me.

Although wildlife agencies and hunting groups are quick to point out the biological advantages of hunting — and it's no less true because of it — I don't hunt because of my desire to control animal populations.

I hunt because I love life.

It may seem a contradiction to love life and take it at the same time, but life is a contradiction sustained from its own consumption, and hunting is as vital to its process as movement is to motion.

Hunting, like everything else, has changed for me over time. It must be connected to place and the primeval beauty of wild country, of which there is precious little left. I make no apologies for my love of hunting. It's been nurtured from a lifetime of finding paths without trails, signs or bridges, sharing only the company of a good dog, a horse, or, if I'm very lucky, a special person like my daughter.

Watching the scene through the blur of tears lost in the pouring rain, I walked up as she stood over the buck.

A sense of wonder overwhelmed her excitement and disbelief as she knelt down and stroked the still-warm body.

Understanding our connection with the earth begins by closing the gap between ourselves and our sustenance. And Susan had just taken her first deliberate step in making that connection.

The torch of hunting had been passed, if she wishes to carry it.

A version of this story was published in the Corvallis, Oregon newspaper. A letter to the Editor came back from a reader who said the story caused a "deep sadness and disbelief." The reader advised Susan to preserve wildlife with a camera and not hunt. Twelve-year-old Susan wrote the following response:

SUSAN AND SCOTT STOUDER WITH SUSAN'S FIRST DEER.

Dear Editor,

I'm the girl who was in the Gazette-Times with the deer. I read the letter to the editor that said I should preserve the beauty of wildlife with a camera.

I know a camera preserves memories, but I don't know how it preserves wildlife. Hunting, by itself, doesn't preserve wildlife either. But hunting with my father lets me understand preservation.

I've seen cattle and chickens penned for slaughter like they have no feelings. I've seen miles and miles of land cleared for crops where no animal can live. My family lives on wild deer and elk meat. Deer and elk live like animals were meant to live — wild and free.

Hunting for them where they live is preservation to me.

We all kill to eat. We kill by shopping in a grocery store. We kill by building houses where animals live. We kill by draining water and clearing land to grow crops. And we kill by making millions of miles of highways and millions of trucks to bring those crops to us.

The "deep sadness and disbelief" that was mentioned [by the reader who wrote the letter] should be felt. It should be felt every time we think about what we do every day.

Susan Stouder

Land, then, is not merely soil; it is a fountain of energy flowing through a circuit of soils, plants and animals.

ALDO LEOPOLD[3]

CHAPTER 9

Codes of Behavior

*There is an order which prohibits every person throughout all the
countries subject to the Great Khan from daring to kill hares, roebucks,
fallow deer, stags or animals of that kind, or any large birds, between the
months of March and October. This is that they may increase and
multiply; and as the breadth of this order is attended by punishment,
game of every description increases prodigiously.*

MARCO POLO[1]

Since the days of Kublai Khan, hunters have placed certain restrictions on themselves such as seasons, limits and methods. Some of the earliest game laws were religious, as in Deuteronomy XXII, where one finds the prohibition: Do not take birds from their nests.

Arriving in the United States, where land was free, game abounded for anyone's taking and no one worried about habitat loss; there were early hunting excesses that mark a sad page in American history. Sailors invaded the breeding grounds and wiped out the great auk and the Labrador duck. The chicken-like heath hen was forced to extinction by market hunting, destruction of habitat by agricultural expansion and the introduction of domestic cats. The near extinction of the American bison, the wild turkey and the elk were directly related to the economic value of their flesh and the absence of any laws to curb excess (and in the case of bison, of a U.S. military strategy designed to subdue Native Americans).

The bison's decline from a herd of 60 million that nearly covered the entire North American continent when Europeans first set foot on American soil to less than 100 in the wild in 1900 was, in the end, a purposeful act. Many Indian tribes were dependent on the buffalo for food. So long as they had food, they would, and could, resist European advances. Deprived of their food and of the central figure in their religious beliefs, Indians migrated to reservations to avoid starvation. To hasten the end of the Indian wars, the Army gave away ammunition to market hunters, opposed any restrictions on killing buffalo, and set fire to large sections of prairie to kill off animals or take away their forage so they would starve.

The passenger pigeon, once the most abundant larger bird in the world, and certainly the most abundant edible bird, became extinct in the early 1900s. It is hard to fathom the abundance of this large relative of the mourning dove, but one late 1800s hunt by market hunters of the Petoskey flock in northern Michigan supposedly resulted in 100 million dead birds, which were packed in barrels and shipped by rail across the country. At one time, passenger pigeon was the most popular and affordable meat on the market in the United States.

For today's hunters there are laws and there are ethics that go beyond laws. One I was taught by my father was that you should never shoot a porcupine because it is the one animal that a man, lost in the woods without a gun, could catch and kill for food with just a rock or a stick.

Another ethical standard, proposed by the International Bowhunter Education Foundation, applies to ownership of an animal that has been previously wounded by someone else. If the wounded animal has been mortally wounded but is not dead and is shot again by a second hunter, the game should be given to the first hunter, even if the second hunter administered the killing shot.

Europe has a much longer tradition of sport hunting than North America, and consequently, a rich heritage of hunting customs. Colonel Craig Boddington explains some of the European rules and regulations that preserve game animals, as well as the etiquette of the hunt:

The Last Bite

BY COLONEL CRAIG BODDINGTON, USMCR

Other continents have recently surpassed Europe in human population, but western Europe is actually a very small place compared with the vastness of Africa, Asia, and the Americas. She [Europe] has been settled — what we might call civilized — for many centuries. Her agriculture is intensive, and all of her natural resources are exploited to their fullest. And yet, in the patchwork of farms and towns large and small that extend from Scandinavia to Italy and from western Russia to Portugal, Europe also boasts amazingly large healthy populations of a diverse array of wildlife. There are wild ducks and geese in the wetlands, along with grouse, partridge, and rabbits in the fields — and more. Dainty roebuck thrive in the edge habitats created by agriculture. Wild boar and red deer roam the forests, and the mountains are home to several varieties of chamois and ibex. Still more European moose abound in the northern forests, and reindeer roam the tundras of Lapland. Even a few brown bears and wolves still persist in more remote regions.

All of this is in spite of — very possibly because of — centuries of intensive hunting. European hunting is rich in tradition, much of which goes against the grain of North American hunting tradition. In 1776, we Americans established the basic premise of public stewardship of wildlife. The European tradition evolved several centuries ago. Even then it was clear to the ruling monarchies that there wasn't enough game for everyone. So the solution was simple. Ownership of wildlife, and the prerogative to hunt, rested with the aristocracy. The American Constitution was largely reactionary, and one of its reactions was to do away with the trappings of monarchy — including hunting as the exclusive province of the ruling class.

So we have developed as a society that considers hunting a basic privilege — if not right — of every citizen. Although the European monarchies are either long gone or relegated to ceremonial status, the European tradition of hunting as the province of the favored few continues. Today, however, this is not by birthright, but by economic reality. There is not enough open land, nor enough wildlife, for public hunting in Europe as we know it in the United States — not a thousand years ago, and certainly not today. So, Europe maintains a system of privatizations of wildlife, and that wildlife has significant value. Hunting is the province of the landowners . . . and those who can afford to pay the landowners for the privilege.

It is expensive, and it is also complex, with conventions varying from country to country. Nowhere are the traditions stronger than in the Germanic countries — Germany and Austria, with much of the tradition carried throughout Switzerland, Hungary, the Czech and Slovak Republics, and Poland. Throughout the region, hunters are small in number compared to the overall population, but despite this the anti-hunting sentiment is small and hunters are accorded significant respect. In large measure this is because they earn it. The requirements to obtain a hunting license vary significantly, but nowhere in Europe is it a simple matter of attending a perfunctory hunter safety course and plunking down a few bucks (or francs or shillings). In Germany and Austria, weeks of classroom and field study are followed by serious and intensive exams, both written and practical. The prospective hunter must know the firearms and hunting laws — and he must know the game as well. A shooting test is also common, for wounded animals are simply not tolerated. In Germany, this testing is very much a one-shot affair: You may sit the exam only once, and if you fail, you may hunt in other countries, but you will never hunt in your native land.

Through license fees, trophy fees, and lease fees, it is the amateur sportsman who pays for Europe's intensive wildlife management. However, it is the gamekeeper who conducts this management, charged with not only maintaining the wildlife, but maintaining the traditions of the hunt. Not all lands are private; there are forests held by federal, provincial and local governments. Most are hunted in some fashion, with the rights leased to individuals, groups or permits allocated by drawing. Virtually all lands that have wildlife are under the care of a gamekeeper, called jaeger in the Germanic countries. This is an honored profession. In times gone by, the mantle of jaeger was passed down through the generations. Today, most younger jaegers will have the equivalent of a degree in wildlife management.

It is the jaeger's job to ensure that the interests of the game are looked after. This is often not easy, for most lands in Europe are very much multiple-use. One evening in Austria I sat in a hochsitz, an elevated blind, above a small road that overlooked a lovely meadow. In the late afternoon, the hikers and bikers passed underneath us after spending a day in the mountains. As evening neared, a herdsman brought several dozen cattle underneath us, driving them into a corral nearer to town. And after everything settled down, the red deer began moving into the meadow.

The jaeger literally lives with the game, ensuring the habitat is maintained and establishing hunting quotas to maintain the optimum herd balance. This, too, is far more intensive in Europe than any other part of the world. The harvest is carefully managed by age group and sex. Younger animals that are harvested will almost invariably have imperfect antlers that would never reach full development; middle-aged animals with potential for greatness are not harvested. For instance, a Klass Eine (Class One) red stag will be more than 12 years old, past his prime and having had the opportunity to pass his genes along. I have been fortunate to hold Class One permits. In the search for such a stag, I have been tantalized by awesome creatures that were simply too young — eight-, nine-, and ten-year-old prime stags that must be allowed to continue to breed.

A local hunter who has attended the schooling is expected to know the difference. If he has a license for a young stag, a Class Three, this is what he will take. If he has a license for Class Two-B, he must take a middle-aged stag with irregular points — and woe

to him if he takes a Class Two-A, a middle-aged stag with perfect conformation. Depending on the country, accommodations are made for visiting foreigners. Whether a local sportsman or a visitor, however, most hunters in Europe are accompanied by the jaeger. Regardless of who the hunter is and who is paying the bill, the convention is that the jaeger's word is law.

On his shoulders rests the decision as to whether a given animal is suitable for the allocated license. On his shoulders, too, rests the shoot/don't shoot decision. There is little long-range shooting in Europe, and still less chancy shots at running game. Once a decision to harvest is made, the hunter and the jaeger share the responsibility to make a clean, efficient kill. Given the circumstances, this is not so difficult as it sounds. Game in Europe is harvested in an efficient, surgical fashion; there is no pressure from hordes of orange-coated nimrods combing the fields. There are no guarantees. The jaeger will know generally where to look for a certain animal that fits the allocated license, but the game is not fenced. It may take days to find the right animal . . . and he may not ever be found. Usually, however, the harvest is successful. And it is a harvest, with the venison going to market, not into the freezer of the hunter.

The jaeger literally raises the game, seeing the animals from birth to maturity and ultimately to the table. His charge is not only management of the game, but also management of the hunter as the harvesting tool. Instilled in his being is respect for the land and the animals. He must ensure that the proper animal is found and dispatched humanely, and it is his charge to preside over a final ceremony to honor the fallen beast. When an animal is taken, the occasion is initially solemn — the congratulations, backslapping, and sharing of schnapps can come later. First the jaeger will break off a green twig, then break it again in

CRAIG BODDINGTON WITH STAG, AND "LAST BITE" SPRIG IN HIS HAT AND STAG'S MOUTH.

two. The first part is gently placed in the animal's mouth, "the last bite." The second part is dipped gently in the animal's blood. Then the jaeger removes his hat, places the twig upon it, and passes it to the hunter with his left hand. He will say solemnly, "Waismannsheil," the hunter's salute.

The hunter will remove his hat and accept the bloodied twig with his left hand, placing it on his hat and replying, "Waidmannsdank," the hunter's thanks. And then, having paid homage to a fine creature, the celebrating may commence.

Driven hunts, whose beginnings and ends are signaled by sounding a hunting horn, have been conducted since before the arrival of gunpowder from Asia. At the end of the day's driven hunt, game taken is laid out in a special pattern, and the jaeger honors both hunters and animals.

Intensive management, selective harvest, respect for the animal — these are the cornerstones that have kept European hunting alive throughout this past millennium. Still, the European hunter has problems. His sport is increasingly expensive, and he is a small and insignificant part of the European population. Much of his system could not work at this late date in North America, nor would we want our sport to be as exclusive as his must be. But we could learn much from him, and it is encapsulated in a simple bumper sticker I saw in Austria: "Ohne Jaeger, Kein Wild." "Without hunters, no wild game." We say similar things in North America, but in much of Europe the nonhunting population believes this truth.

'Frevel' belongs to the same word group as the English word 'frivolous.' It has the same nuance but means more than just a frivolous attitude. In modern German, 'frevel' means trespassing beyond certain not so much legal as common rules of behavior. We mostly use it now in association with hunting. 'Jagfrevel' is the usual word, and there it means 'transgressing the hunting rules,' shooting pregnant deer or hunting in the closed season, for instance, or shooting badly and wounding without killing, and then not bothering about the wounded animal afterward. . . In former times it had a more religious connotation and approached the meaning of blasphemy (sacrilege); spitting in the church or such could be called 'frevelish.' 'Frevel' meant stepping over the border, going beyond a respectful attitude toward the numinous powers."

MARIE-LOUISE VON FRANZ[2]

Religious Laws of Hunting

Religions often spell out specific codes of behavior to follow when engaged in some kind of special practice. In the Christian tradition, following the great flood, in Genesis 10:9 the Bible says of Nimrod, a descendent of Noe, that "He was a mighty hunter before the Lord; that's why it is said, 'Like Nimrod, a mighty hunter before the Lord.' " Esau, the son of Isaac, is also described as a "skillful hunter" in Genesis 25:27, sent by his father to hunt for an animal that will provide savory meat (Genesis 27:3-4). The Israelites were instructed in Deuteronomy 12:15 and 14:15 as to what kinds of wildlife were permissible to eat: "the deer, the gazelle, the roe deer, the wild goat, the ibex, the antelope, and the mountain sheep."

Seeking guidance from The Bible on the righteousness of hunting, Christian hunters point to two key themes. In Genesis 9:3, God instructs Noah, "Every moving thing that liveth shall be meat for you." As hunting weapons are described, hunters such as Esau and Nimrod are honored, and guidance is given about treatment of animals and food, one can conclude that the teachings of The Bible clearly support hunting. Secondly, in numerous places, such as Gen. 1:1-31; Gen. 9:2, 3; Gen. 10:9; Gen. 27:3, man is given dominion over the earth, to partake of, and govern all its

STATUE OF ST. HUBERT
St. Hubert, the patron saint of hunting, is associated with many Catholic parishes as well as hotels and military units. This statue of the saint is from St. Hubert's Catholic Church in Chanhassen, Minnesota. The church's newsletter is appropriately named "The Hunter."

resources wisely. These passages and others are interpreted to mean that all life is created in God's image and man has a stewardship responsibility that should be guided by religious ethics, as in Genesis 2:15: "The Lord God took the man and put him in the Garden of Eden to dress it and tend it."

The Bible also pays special attention to blood in the preparation of game for, "Life of the flesh is in the blood." In olden days, blood was sometimes sacrificed on the altar, so it was seen as holy and people were forbidden to eat it. In Leviticus 17:13, the instructions are given that: "Any man also of the people of Israel, or of strangers that sojourn amoung them, who takes in hunting any beast or bird that may be eaten shall pour out its blood and cover it with dust."

Archery, nets, spears and pits are described as methods of hunting, and Proverbs 12:27 gives the following guidance on cooking, "The lazy man does not roast his game, but the diligent man prizes his possessions."

The Code of Canon Law of the Catholic Church says that priests may hunt, but with restraint, and forbids them from engaging in "noisy hunting," (i.e. with dogs). The reason is not that the Catholic church opposes hunting as sinful, for it does not consider hunting as sin at all, but that it believes hunting does not conform with the proper decorum of the clergy. Non-Catholic Christian clergy, in general, are free to hunt, and some become guides and outfitters.

There are a number of Christian hunters' organizations. One way they suggest to bring your faith along when you go hunting is to take a Bible with you into the field and read it as you are waiting in your blind.

Muslim Laws of the Hunt

There is a long, rich tradition of hunting in Muslim countries. The prophet Mohammed practiced archery, hunted, and advocated others to practice archery because it would be good for them. Like Zen masters of the east, Muslims apply principles of meditation to archery, making them some of the finest archers in the world. They also hunt with falcons, a practice that is thought to have originated in India.

Muslims consider hunting a holy craft, and trace its practice back to the prophet Ishmael, who was a great hunter. Among the mystical Sufi tradition of the Middle East, hunters were organized into guilds, which hunted according to chivalric rituals. There is a Sufi story that is quite similar to the legend of Saint Hubert. A hunter goes out into the forest, comes upon a deer, and starts to shoot, only to have the deer change into a dervish (a spiritual teacher) who admonishes the hunter for not following the proper code of conduct of Islamic law. That hunter subsequently went on to become a famous Sufi saint.

Muslims believe that hunting is proper only according to the heavenly principles of mercy, moderation and leniency. In olden days, scholars and religious teachers might accompany royal hunting parties to ensure that animals were hunted only according to a strict code, which was part of a much larger body of rules for righteous conduct called The Islamic Laws of Contracts. The Islamic Laws, including those that prescribe methods of hunting, killing and slaughtering, have been passed down over the ages. Interpreted by leaders of the various schools, they continue to guide modern Muslim hunters.

With the permission of the World Federation of Khoja Shia Ithnaasheri (KSI) Muslim Communities comes the following selection of instructions from *Islamic Laws According to Fatawa of Ayatullah* on how to hunt *halal*, or in a righteous way that is acceptable to Allah. Abiding by these laws results in harvesting meat that is pure, *Pak*. If a Muslim does not hunt in the manner prescribed by the Laws, then eating the meat is forbidden, *haraam*. And Mohammed did not approve of shooting animals that one does not eat, unless it is to protect domestic animals.

Islamic Laws According to Fatawa of Ayatullah

2593. If a wild animal like deer, partridge, and wild goat whose meat is halal to eat, or a halal animal which was once a domestic one but later turned wild, like a cow or a camel, which runs away and becomes wild, is hunted in accordance with the laws which will be explained later, it is Pak and halal to eat. But a domestic animal like sheep or fowl whose meat is halal to eat does not become Pak and halal by hunting.

2594. A wild animal whose meat is halal to eat becomes Pak and halal to eat by hunting if it is capable of running away or flying. Based on this, the young of deer which cannot run away, and the young one of a partridge which cannot fly, do not become Pak and halal to eat by hunting. And if a deer and its young one which cannot run are hunted with one bullet, the deer will be halal but its young one will be haraam to eat.

2597. Dogs and pigs do not become Pak by slaughtering and hunting and it is also haraam to eat their meat. And if a flesh-eating animal like wolf or leopard is slaughtered in the manner which will be mentioned later, or is hunted by means of a bullet, etc., it is Pak, but its meat does not become halal for consumption. And if it is hunted down by a hunting dog, then its body cannot be considered Pak.

2610. If a halal wild animal is hunted with a weapon and it dies, it becomes halal, and its body becomes Pak, if the following five conditions are fulfilled:

(i) The weapon used for hunting should be able to cut through, like a knife or a sword, or should be sharp, like a spear or an arrow, so that due to its sharpness, it may tear the body of the animal. If an animal is hunted with a trap, or hit by a piece of wood or a stone, it does not become Pak, and it is haraam to eat its meat. And if an animal is hunted with a gun and its bullet is so fast that it pierces into the body of the animal and tears it up, the animal will be Pak and halal, but if the bullet is not fast enough and enters the body with pressure and kills, or burns its body with heat, and the animal dies due to that heat, it is a matter of Ishkal to say that the animal is Pak or halal.

(ii) The hunter should be a Muslim or at least a Muslim child who can distinguish between good and bad.

(iii) The hunter should aim the weapon for hunting at the particular animal. Therefore, if a person takes aim at some target, and kills an animal accidentally, that animal will not be Pak and it will be haraam to eat its meat.

(iv) While using the weapon, the hunter should recite the name of Allah, and it is sufficient if he utters the name of Allah before the target is hit. But if he does not recite Allah's name intentionally, the animal does not become halal. There is, however, no harm if he fails to do so because of forgetfulness.

(v) The animal will be haraam if the hunter reaches it when it is already dead, or, even if it is alive, he has no time left to slaughter it. And if he has enough time to slaughter it and he does not slaughter it till it dies, it will be haraam.

2633. All birds, like eagle, vultures and wild falcons having claw and talon, are haraam to eat. And all such birds whose gliding is more than flapping the wings, and have talons, are also haraam to eat. Those whose flapping of the wings while flying are more than gliding, are halal to eat. Thus, one can identify halal birds from haraam ones by observing how they fly. And if the style of a bird's flight cannot be determined, that bird will be considered halal for eating if it has a crop or gizzard or a spur on the back of its feet. In the absence of all these, the bird will be haraam. As an obligatory precaution, one should refrain from eating the meat of all types of crows. Other birds like hens, the pigeons, the sparrows, and including the ostrich and the peacock are halal to eat, but it is Makrooh to kill birds like swallows and hoopoes. [Makrooh means literally "it is better not to do this, but not forbidden."] And the animals which fly, but are not classified as winged birds, like the bats, are haraam; similarly, the bees, the mosquitoes, and other flying insects are, as an obligatory precaution, haraam.

None of the major religions of the world prohibit followers from hunting. Religions that follow Asian traditions, such as Hinduism and Buddhism where the Ahimsa tradition is honored (Ahimsa literally means "do not harm") may not be able to kill animals they eat, but they can raise them and eat them. The East Indian holy book, *The Rig Veda*, states clearly that so long as one is spiritually pure, eating anything is permissible.

Perhaps no one has better described the ethic that should guide all hunting laws than biologist-philosopher Aldo Leopold, who said in his classic work *A Sand County Almanac*: "A thing is right when it tends to preserve the integrity, stability and beauty of the biotic community. It is wrong when it tends to do otherwise."[3]

Leopold was the founder of modern wildlife management science, which has provided the scientific background for wildlife law enforced today by state and federal game wardens. Game wardens are police officers whose duty is to protect fish and wildlife. They are a rare species. There are more police officers in New York City than there are game wardens in the entire United States.

A common feeling of people when approached by a law enforcement officer is, "What have I done wrong now?" This negative image of officers makes their job even more difficult and dangerous, and during hunting season nearly all those individuals approached by wardens are armed. The State of California has instituted a program to try to help elevate the public image of game wardens

THEODORE ROOSEVELT WITH POACHERS (CIRCA 1880S, DAKOTA TERRITORY)
In African Game Trails, *Theodore Roosevelt said, "Game butchery is as objectionable as any other form of wanton cruelty or barbarity; but to protest against all hunting is a sign of softness of head, not soundness of heart." This photo of Roosevelt holding some poachers was taken during his ranching years in Dakota Territory, circa 1880s, when he was a deputy sheriff. Roosevelt always had a strong feeling for justice, which is reflected in his famous slogan for foreign policy, "Speak softly, and carry a big stick."*

and encourage good hunter behavior. Wardens who see hunters performing good acts of sportsmanship in the field may stop them and issue Caught Doing Good certificates. At the end of the hunting season, the names of all the hunters who have been issued positive certificates are placed in a drawing. Winners receive prizes of sporting goods.

For a subsistence hunter, for whom success is often a life or death matter, methods of taking wild animals are determined by practicality, with little thought to sport. Native hunters might use nets, snares, deadfalls or pit traps, or even kill entire herds of animals like bison by setting grass fires and stampeding them over a cliff. Hunting ducks and geese when they are molting and flightless is certainly more likely to be successful than when they can fly. All such methods are illegal to the modern hunter, who must follow a code of laws, and hopefully, a code of ethics. The modern ethics of pursuit were set down in a code of conduct by Theodore Roosevelt and a small group of his friends in the rules of the premier big game hunting society of America, the Boone and Crockett Club:

> The term 'fair chase' shall not be held to include killing bear, wolf, or cougar in traps, nor 'fire-hunting,' nor 'crusting' moose, elk, or deer in deep snow, nor killing game from a boat while it is swimming in the water.[4]

With the passing of time and the advent of new technologies, fair chase is now expanded. It is defined by the Boone and Crockett Club as "the ethical, sportsmanlike, and lawful pursuit and taking of any free-ranging wild game animal that does not give the hunter an improper or unfair advantage over such game animals." The following methods of taking game are now defined as unfair chase.

I. Spotting or herding game from the air, followed by landing in its vicinity for the purpose of pursuit and shooting.

II. Herding, pursuing, or shooting game from any motorboat or motor driven vehicle.

III. Use of electronic devices for attracting, locating, or observing game, or for guiding the hunter to such game.

IV. Hunting game confined by artificial barriers, including escape-proof fenced enclosures, or hunting game transplanted for the purpose of commercial shooting.

V. Taking of game in a manner not in compliance with the game laws or regulations of the federal government or of any state, province, territory, or tribal council on reservation lands.

CHAPTER 10

The Call

*The primitive man's belief that the bear dance will inevitably bring
the bear to the hunt depends on . . . [an] unconscious identity, for
the bear and man are felt to be in a continuum. And it must be
admitted that sometimes the bear seems to feel it too, since reliable
observers have stated that the bear does come when so called.*

ESTHER HARDING[1]

It may be the alarm clock that finally turns the hunter out of bed, but long before that annoying sound, voices of the hunt have been calling, kicking in a progressive buildup of natural chemicals of excited anticipation — the hunter's high. The desire to hunt begins to well up long before the hunter sets foot in the field. The moon passing overhead, the calls of migrating geese, the leaves turning color, bucks shedding velvet from their antlers, or a cool breeze: all speak directly to the soul, awakening to the hunt the bear or big cat within each of us. So it is with instincts. They awaken from deep thickets of the psyche, moving upward to consciousness like fog, springs, perhaps even wildfire. In their path, chemistry is stirred. Changes in mind, body and emotion unfold.

Children all around the world are drawn to hunt animals in their play. No one has to teach them to do it. It comes naturally. It is an

instinct that can be acknowledged and developed into a passionate complex of skills, or it can be thrust back into the unconscious. The choice is individual, influenced by culture.

Uninhibited by culture, some people come to hunting as a calling. Following their instinctual voices, the hunt changes their lives, sometimes moving then to develop hobbies that in turn become passions in their own right.

The powerful energies of the hunt move us to plan, prepare and create. For Ragnar Insulandar of Sweden, the hunter's instinct is strong. Inspired by meeting the Saami, or Lapps, he has become a skilled artisan, recreating the traditional Saami archery equipment, as well as studying the hunting culture from which it arose.

KWAKIUTL CHIEF MUNGO MARTIN DRUMMING AND CHANTING. THE KWAKIUTLS BELIEVE THAT THE SOULS OF DECEASED GREAT HUNTERS BECOME KILLER WHALES IN THEIR NEXT LIVES.

The Saami, the Bow and the Great Hunger

BY RAGNAR INSULANDER

Ever since my youth, when I made several weeklong treks through the Swedish mountains together with my father, the Saami country in the far north (Lappland) has held a special attraction for me. To remove my watch and put it at the bottom of the backpack and to wander freely in the wilderness far from all marked trails; to meet bears, but no humans; to watch the sun-dappled mountain meadows; to find the red tufts of Moss Campion and Purple Saxifrage—all this gave a deep satisfaction to my soul and nourished a vision of the free life which has inspired me.

The image of a people in harmony with the land where they live has served me as a guiding force, professionally and personally. I am not Saami, but as I am Swedish, I believe understanding their culture offers wisdom that applies to healing the soul of modern man in general. To understand a native culture, intellectual study alone is not enough; one has to walk a bit in their footsteps, and so I have studied their beliefs about hunting and their weapons.

The Saami Bow from the Vibby-bog

The Saami were known as great archers. The bow — jouks — is said to have been strong. In a folk song from the Faroe Islands, even the Viking king Odin carries a Saami bow.

Archery was very popular among the Saami until the 18th century, when crossbows and firearms prevailed. Young boys had to practice every day. The target was a piece of birch bark at the top of a pole. They had to hit the target to get something to eat.

There are only a handful of finds of old Saami bows from Scandinavia. The most beautiful is perhaps the bow from the Vibby bog in The National Museum of History in Stockholm, where it can be seen in the permanent exhibition. It has been dated to 900 ± 70 BP [Before the Present Time, or 900 years ago]. As in the case with all the other finds, only the 126-centimeter-long belly has been preserved. The wood is compression wood from pine (*Pinus silvestris*). The belly has some lines or grooves, which have been incised to reduce the tension in the wood to prevent it from splitting or warping. Besides these approximately one- to two-milllimeter deep grooves, the bow has some additional decorations in a typical Saami pattern. There are also some weak traces of diagonal binding, which indicate that the bow was covered with a thin layer of birch bark.

I examined recent Fenno-Ugrian bows, old texts and illustrations and have come to the following conclusions: The bow originally had static ears that were more or less recurved and the bow was probably somewhat reflexed. The ears were made from the same wooden strip as the back of the bow, or possibly from separate pieces of a third kind of wood (Bird Cherry, *Prunus padus*). The back was made from birch (*Betula alba*) and was flat and thin (0.3 to 0.5 centimeters).

Constructing this bow requires not only knowledge of wood working, but an awareness of nature in general. The compression wood (in Saami, "bye" or "bije") is taken in January and February in the dark of the moon. Preferably the tree should lean to the south or southeast for the best quality compression wood. It is often hard work to cleave the trunk and extract the compression wood, particularily if the trunk is thick. The compression wood easily splits, so it is necessary to wedge the trunk apart before cleaving it out.

The birch wood should be collected at the same season, but under a waxing moon. The fish — the perch needed for boiling to make glue — may be caught almost at any season. The glue is made from the skins. Once the compression wood has been roughly shaped it is tempered over a bed of glowing charcoal and then glued to the birch strip. Then, an approximately six-inch-long ear is glued to each end. Once all this has been done, one has created a new substance, a laminated material with completely new properties.

Once the bow is balanced and has been proof-fired it is covered with birch bark. The bark is stripped from the living tree in swaths several yards long, which is most easily done when the sap is rising in the tree, sometime after midsummer. And then, the finished weapon is in your hands.

* * *

Reindeer are now domesticated, but once they were wild. When the Saami wanted to hunt wild reindeer in winter, they used skis. For balance, they would use a spear in one hand and a special hunting bow with a metal point and woven basket on one end, much like a modern ski pole.

In addition to conventional hunting arrows

tipped with a cutting point, Saami also made special bird hunting arrows with clever designs. One, a whistling arrow, was shot into the air over a flock of flying birds. It looks like and makes a sound resembling an attacking falcon swooping down through the air. I have tried this, and it makes the birds fly down into cover where the hunter can shoot at them more easily. Another special arrow is a skipping arrow for waterfowl hunting. When you shoot it at birds on the water, the arrow keeps skipping along the surface for a long way, so if it misses the first duck or a goose in a flock, it will go on after another.

The Noaidde (shaman) and the bow

The Saami bow is an object of power. In the old days it was kept together with the shaman's drum in the part of the kåta (the Saami teepee) called the påssjo where no woman could enter. When the bow was removed from the kåta it was not taken through the ordinary door but rather through a small opening in the rear of the kåta. The bow and the beliefs connected with it were so important that one might consider them as part of the material and spiritual glue that held Saami society together.

Saami drew their cosmology on the drums. On the drum heads the bow is a recurring theme, particularly as an attribute of the goddess Juksakka and in a variety of hunting scenes. Juksakka or Steuke-edne, was the goddess who once gave the bow to the Saami and taught them to shoot with it. The name means the Bow-Lady or the Bow-Mother. Juksakka and some other goddesses are also connected to childbirth.

It was customary to attach a small bow to the cradle of male children. This was meant to protect the child from malignant spirits and to make the boy a skillful hunter later in life. Miniature bows could also be carried as amulets among the Saami.

Leibolmai, the Saami hunting god, is often depicted with a bow. His name is usually translated as Alder-forest man, Forest-God, or Bear-God. The alder tree, leibbe, is sacred, and from its bark was made the pigment used to paint the signs on the noaddie drums. The bear was also related to the alder forest where grows the herb tolta, which the bear is fond of. It was customary to sacrifice bows and arrows to Leibolmai to ensure good hunting.

The bow was also used as a divination tool. Among the Djagatai, the Schor, and the Altai of Eurasia, the shaman was called by a name that translates as "the seer who uses a bow." The bow acted as a conduit between the shaman and his helping spirits, indicating their will. The Saami noaidde's helping spirit,

SAAMI PLAYING BOW

Passevare-Olmaj, could be contacted in several ways, through the joik (Saami lyrical chanting story-song), with the drum, or through the movements of a gun hanging under the roof of the kåta. It seems reasonable that before they started using a gun it was a bow that was hung in the kåta roof. The answers of the spirits could be read from the way the gun (or bow) swung.

Possibly, the Saami also used the bow as a musical instrument. In many parts of the world it is believed that the bow was the forerunner of stringed instruments like the guitar. A number of cultures have used rhythmic striking or plucking of the bow string to induce trance, much the same as beating on a drum. In a cave from Les Trois Fréres Cave in France, there is a painting representing a man with an animal head (animal mask) playing on a small bow. In front of him are two running animals, the nearest looks like a deer with a bison head, while in front of this is a running reindeer with webbed forefeet. The painting possibly illustrates the ritual that often precedes the actual hunt in shamanistic cultures. This ritual cannot be separated from the hunt; it is rather a spiritual prelude to the actual hunt that generates a relation to the hunted animals as beings with a spirit, a relation that permeates the entire concept of the hunt, the kill, the butchering, and the consumption of the killed animal.

Sarva the Cosmic Moose Hunt

In the shamanistic hunting cultures, the killing of game was in accord with the cosmic order. To kill was actually an act by which the men preserved life, comparable with childbirth for the women. Without hunting and killing, no life was possible. Without game, humans would perish and life cease.

The animals were fellow-beings, in some ways equal to humans, and in some ways actually stronger and more powerful. The animals were not only necessary for food. Through mediation, the shaman could enter the animal stratum of his own soul. In this way the dream time was recreated, the time before time when men and the other animals were not yet sundered. The relation to the animals of power — such as the bear, the moose, the reindeer, or the loon — was both cosmic and initiatory. These animals were both the ancestors of man and the teachers and initiators of the shamans.

Some researchers speak about a myth-complex, The Great Hunt, of which the Saami bear-hunting rituals are an example. Some tales have also been preserved that tell about a cosmic moose hunt called Sarva. Just as here on earth there is a Great Hunt going on in the sky, the stars are actually the moose and its hunters. For the Lule Saami, Cassiopeia was the top of the moose's giant horns, while Perseus was the lower part of the horns and the front of the body, and some of the stars in Auriga were his rear part. The moose was pursued by several hunters, particularly Favta (Arcturus), whose bow is Charles' Wain; Galla and his two sons (the three stars in the Belt of Orion); the Two Skiers (Castor and Pollux); and the Old Lady with the Hunting Dogs (the Pleiades).

The cosmic moose is also a common theme on the drums. On the southern type of drum, it is often centrally placed on one of the four beams of the Sun, where it may be in company with Leibolmai, the Hunting God. The moose was thus a sacred beast, just like the bear and the reindeer, and one of the animals the Saami often jojkade (sang).

In Scandinavia, the Moose is still known as the king of the forest. The sacred moose and the rituals connected with it are probably very old in northern Europe, and seem to be illustrated on rock engravings in northern Norway. On these 5,500-year-old rock engravings, one can discern human figures holding poles with moose heads and performing some sort of a ritual or dance in front of a moose. The same theme is found on the somewhat younger rock engravings at Namforsen in Sweden. Similar poles with moose heads carved from horn have been found in Mesolithic graves near Lake Onega in Carelia.

The Great Hunger and the Little Hunger

From the close relation and the dependence on the animals, a gratitude grew—a gratitude to the animals for giving up their lives in order that men might live and a gratitude to the plants for giving an excess that fed the people. And there was gratitude that the animals allowed themselves to be killed without coming back for revenge. In traditional hunting cultures, this gratitude is expressed in rituals where man in his turn passed his surplus on to higher powers. Matter became transformed and man's rituals, prayer and sacrifices fed the gods, e. g. the Great Mother of all Animals, who in turn provided the game animals. The gods in their turn continually maintained and renewed all creation. In this way the circle is closed, the gods are both at the top and the roots, the world of mankind, animals and plants is in between, and all is part of the same great cycle of being.

This gratitude has all but disappeared in our affluent society. This has led to psychological wounds that I think are an important aspect of the ecological crisis. We have forgotten on a very deep level how to relate to the animals and to nature as a whole. The ecological crisis is a reflection of an inner ecological crisis. In our inner world, the animals have become extinct as living, soulful beings. On the plate, animals have been reduced to carbohydrates, proteins and fats. We eat the same meat as did the men in the traditional societies, but we don't get the same nourishment. The food has lost its spiritual nourishment. Only the Little Hunger is satisfied.

We have broken the spritual food chain; we have broken the contract with the animals and nature. We no longer understand that they have a meaning beyond being food and raw materials for our physical well being. We are hunted by the Great Hunger, and in our blindness we think that even more material riches will appease it.

When hunting with a bow, you must come much closer. This adds richness to the experience, and increases feelings of respect for the animals. This is one way of satisfying our larger hunger. We no longer perform (execute) the rituals, the prayers and hymns. It is time for us to take them up again. This might awaken our humility and gratitude. Otherwise, there is a risk that hunting will just be performed as a shallow pleasure, where the feeling of power over nature is the main experience.

Hunting seduces us away from normal routines. All senses are on alert. Days, weeks, months, maybe years of preparation have been made for this moment. After the alarm clock and the calls of friends, the sounds that bring hunters together are musical instruments: originally drums and flutes, today more often horns. The call is sweet music to a hunter's ear, a crystalline sound that unites so many things into the singularity of the hunt.

Autumn Hunting Spell

Autumn has come.
We are off hunting.
Forest Uncle, do not be angry!
Let me meet the black fox,
*   the white hare, the moor hen,*
*   the hazel hen.*
If I go downstream
*   let me meet the beaver, the otter!*
Bring far near, Forest Uncle
that I may get something to my bag!
If you give, there will be something too.

UDMURT (NORTHERN ASIA),
REC. BEFORE 1888[2]

WINTER HUNTING AMONG THE FINNO-UGRIC NATIVE PEOPLES

CHAPTER 11

Pursuit

In the act of hunting, a man becomes, however briefly, part of nature again.
He returns to the natural state, becomes one with the animal, and is freed from
the burden of his existential split: to be part of nature and to transcend it
by virtue of his consciousness. In stalking the animal, he and the animal become
equals, even though man eventually shows his superiority by use of his weapons.

ERICH FROMM[1]

P hysical prowess, mental alertness, intuition, a dash of luck — and most of all the ability to think like the animal pursued — make for a good tracker. An American Indian hunter once told me that he had been taught to track using his sense of smell. His teacher blindfolded him and made him get down on all fours and smell the ground like a dog until he could distinguish animal odors. We who have blunted our sense of smell may scoff at this, but just as wine tasting is an acquired art, so is the trained nose of a perfume chemist.

Speaking of his Apache teacher Stalking Wolf, noted tracking expert Tom Brown Jr. says:

> *In a single track, he could read not only the biography of the animal that had left its signature, but chapters from the lives of all the others that were bound up with it. Like an archeologist reconstructing an animal from a single bone, he used tracks to piece together elaborate structures of interlocking events. Taken in their entirety, those structures amounted to the entire fabric of the woods.*[2]

Written into his contract during his eight-year stint as the costar of the hit television series *Simon and Simon* was a provision that gave Jameson Parker one week off to go deer hunting. "You don't hunt deer because you love them," Parker says. "You love them as a result of hunting them."

Parker did not grow up in a hunting family, but as a child he loved to spend hours of "delicious freedom" roaming the woods. In his 20s, a friend took him hunting. The friend shot a deer. After waiting the appropriate half an hour for the animal to quietly bleed to death, they began to track the blood trail. Of that experience, Parker says, "Something took over that I didn't know I had in me. I tracked that deer on hands and knees. Some other hunters got the deer, but I was hooked for life."

Among native hunters, typically there are acts of preparation for the hunt that not only cleanse the body and remove telltale odors, but also purify the hunter's mind so he or she undertakes the hunt with sincerity of purpose. Smudging oneself with smoke is one of the most common traditional purification rites; not just any smoke, but the smoke of certain herbs that supposedly have special powers beyond the camouflage of odor. Sweet grass, cedar, sage and alder are used for smudging by various Native Americans. Among the Ob-Ugric of northern Asia, who believe that man and the bear are descended from the same ancestor, hunters purify themselves with the smoke of burning birch bark before going hunting. In the native view, when one smudges, not only does the smoke cover telltale human odors, but it also invokes the spirits of the plant people to enjoin with the energies of the hunt, providing additional support and protection from that world to this mundane one.

Smudging with smoke of special plants, like birch bark, is a common native purification ritual prior to the hunt. The smoke is said to purify the mind as well as conceal human odors.

In addition to laws and ethics, some modern hunters purposefully limit themselves. Some say this gives the animals more of a chance. Others maintain it presents a larger challenge to the hunter. Probably, both are true, but limiting one's technologies also enriches the experience of hunting, forcing the hunter into closer sympathy with the animals, which charges the experience with a wild spirit, and makes success even more meaningful. Outfitter/guide Jim Shockey of British Columbia hunts big game with a single-shot, .50-caliber muzzleloading rifle. One shot has to do the trick, and his effective range is much less than with a conventional rifle.

Physical strength, agility, patience, acuity of senses, skilled marksmanship, knowledge of the terrain, and many more skills are all factored into the success of the hunter. But perhaps above all else, being at the right place at the right time is the key to being successful.

Synchronicity. If intuition is an unconscious externalization of the mind that pulls us to situations, then we are always sensing the world around us. So are the animals. How the hunter and the hunted come together is one of life's wonders. As the following story by Jim Shockey suggests, a little natural magic may favor synchronous connections.

It is the strict circumscription of hunting and fishing — those unwritten rules of ethics, etiquette and propriety — that define the challenge . . . Success when it comes must be difficult and uncertain . . . .

Even in the best of times there is an element of difficulty, doubt, discomfort, disappointment, and even danger involved in such pursuits. And often, great distances must be covered during very early hours, even in the dark night.

JIMMY CARTER[3]

Where Tradition, Legend & Reality Meet

Leather creaked and horses' hooves clopped; the hobble chains around my own horse's neck ca-chinged. Clop . . . ca-ching. These most natural of a cappella rhythms followed us down the mountain trail, soothing the pain of lost opportunity. Clop . . . ca-ching. Clop . . . ca-ching.

Bobby Jackson, my Beaver Indian guide, I knew, would soon join in with his singing voice. He'd been singing for the six days that we'd been riding together, and I'd not only become accustomed to his mellifluous tones, I'd also come to enjoy them. He was talented. In another place, he might actually have been discovered. Not much chance of that where we were though, a few hundred miles from civilization in the famed Prophet-Muskwa River drainage of British Columbia.

I'd booked the combination stone sheep and elk hunt after speaking for several years to outfitter Kevin Olmstead and his wife, Victoria. Kevin assured me that not only did his territory hold some of the world's largest stone sheep, it also held more than its fair share of bull elk — facts that my research confirmed were true.

It didn't take much research either. A quick read through the record book was like taking a trip in time back through the illustrious history of stone sheep hunting. The Prophet/Muskwa drainage's most famous inhabitant of course was the Chadwick ram, the largest stone sheep ever killed by a hunter. It was taken in 1936 by S.L. Chadwick and was, according to Kevin, taken from the same base camp that I'd flown into from Fort St. John.

Listen, people, to a story
That was written long ago.

Bobby's dulcet tones, flavored first with a cowboy twang and then uniquely modified with his high-octave Native inflection, rose into the darkening evening.

On the mountain lies a treasure,
Buried deep beneath the snow.

We'd seen a big ram earlier that evening, across a valley, too far to go after that day. To see such a ram, so close, but so proverbially far was a disappointment, or it was to me at least. Bobby hadn't seemed the least bit concerned when we called it a day, packed our horses, and headed back down to spike camp.

And the valley people swore,
They'd have it for their very own.

By the time we reached camp, the stars were in full bloom and the night's cold crawled like a snake across my skin. I shivered and hunched closer to the campfire. I didn't feel like eating much, far too dispirited was I to enjoy the repast.

"Think he'll be there tomorrow?" I asked almost as much to myself as I did to Bobby.

He poked at the fire, moving the coals around. "Sure he will, pardner."

Good enough for me.

For a time, neither one of us spoke, choosing instead to slip into a deep fascination with the flames. It's like that when you're tired and sitting in front of a campfire. The flames wave and flit like Solid Gold dancers, commanding your eyes to follow their lead, to dance *pas de deux*. In the near distance, somewhere in the dark cliffs lining the Prophet River, my ram lay bedded.

"Pardner?" Bobby eventually spoke, without lifting his eyes from the flames.

"Ya."

"You like that ram?"

"Hummmmm." I confirmed.

"Then tomorrow, we'll get him." Bobby threw his stick on the fire and pushed up. "We'll smudge."

"Hmmmm." I wasn't really listening, still

lost as I was in rapt fascination with the flames.

It was later, after the last dark spark popped off like a shooting star into the pitch darkness, that I finally rose and followed Bobby to our small backpack tent. As I crawled through the door flap, I frowned. The tent was fogged with smoke and scented with wild, unnamed herbs. Bobby Jackson sat cross-legged on one side of the tent, across from a tiny flame burning in the lid of a can. He was bidding me to sit across the tent from him.

I did so.

To be sure, the tent wasn't a willow bough sweat lodge, but for this spiritual smudging it was going to have to do.

"Wash with the smoke, pardner." Bobby pulled the smoke over his upper torso. "Make a wish and it will come true."

I did so.

The waving motion caused the small flame, our only light, to waver and flit. Huge shadows crazed across the tent wall behind Bobby, and I assume, behind me. Eerie shadows changed Bobby's facial features and suddenly, in that place, for that time, he wasn't just my hunting guide, he was wisdom, he was a medicine man.

He told me then of the elders, of his people and the truth of the land. He told me stories of healing and healers. He pointed over my shoulder at the tent wall and told me about an ancient white cross on a mountain "over there," a sacred place where the ancient ones had been. He talked of hunting and trapping and he talked about the morrow's hunt.

"Smudging will make it happen." It was all Bobby said to me.

And so smudge we did. Bobby burned the sacred grasses he'd traded from some medicine man whose name I can't recall, and I, the outlander, cleansed myself. As Bobby the storyteller told, the winds whistled high above in the mountain passes. The creek rushed and,

Jim Shockey with Ram

maybe it was in my dreams, but that night a wolf howled. Later — I can't honestly say how much later — I awoke once and saw Bobby, still sitting cross-legged, outlined in the blackness. Then, I slept like the dead.

In this house of dreams,
that you walk like a ghost unseen . . .

The sun didn't rise as early as Bobby did. Out in the blackness, I could hear him quietly singing while he rustled about preparing breakfast. Even through the tent wall, I could smell the cowboy coffee roiling, hear it hissing. Time wasn't wasting exactly and my sleeping bag held me as surely as fate held the day in store.

I allowed myself to slip back into the semi-aware world of coffee-smell induced nostalgia. How many of the old-time sheep hunters had lain in their down bags and smelled the coffee in this very camp spot? Did old John Caputo Sr. hunt here? How about my vote for the greatest hunter ever, Basil Bradbury, or his mentor Herb Klein?

Certainly the godfather of sheep hunting, Jack O'Connor, must have sipped his slightly more powerful version of cowboy coffee here, or close by. And what about the legendary writer Grancel Fitz, the man who, in terms of sheep, coined the phrase "Grand Slam" for taking each of the five species of wild sheep of the world? Had he hunted in this drainage? On this mountain?

"Hey, pardner?" Bobby poked his head in the tent. "Ready to go get your sheep?"

At sun up, we climbed upon our horses and trailed up the mountain again. Eventually we tied the horses up and hiked to the high vantage point where we'd been sitting when we spotted the sheep the evening before. Then we glassed… And glassed.

I spoke first.

"The ram's gone."

And it was. The mountainside he'd been feeding on the evening before was empty, devoid of life. Devoid as I was of hope.

"He'll come." Bobby never doubted for a moment. "Don't worry, he'll come. We smudged."

And come he did. At the stroke of high noon the magnificent ram walked from around the mountain right to where we'd seen him the day before. Was it luck? Or was it big medicine?

The stalk was anticlimatic really; seemingly preordained in some explicable way. We hiked down our side of the valley and up the far slope, using the conveniently placed boulders and ridges to advantage. At 80 yards, I poked my Knight muzzleloader over a rock pile and found the ram in the scope. He was staring at me, for all the world looking like he was expecting someone. BOOM! The deep mysteries involved in the hunt disappeared in a cloud of smoke.

"Pardner?" Bobby was smiling ear to ear. "You just got yourself one fine ram, pardner."

An understatement to be sure. The ram was easily larger than the muzzleloading world record stone sheep. Bobby and I paid last respects to the ram before dressing it and heading downhill. By the next day we were on our way back to Kevin's closest base camp. Bobby sang the whole way.

Concealment

Getting close is what hunting is all about — getting close enough for your shot to be clear, safe and lethal. Clothing, blinds and treestands seek to blend hunters with the pattern of vegetation so that they disappear. Aside from the excitement of the arrival of what you are hunting, the hidden hunter is treated to a continual show, presented by all the other animals that assume no human is around. Having a sparrow land on your shoulder or a rabbit hop across your foot, and not detect you, is a gift you will never forget.

The waterfowl hunter in open waters has a double challenge: staying warm and dry, and keeping concealed so ducks or geese will fly into range. On Lake Erie, duck hunters use pumpkinseed-shaped, one- or two-man layout boats that ride barely above the surface. Painted gray, the boats match the water on a cloudy November day. The hunter covers himself with a gray blanket of canvas, sitting up only to shoot. At 150 yards away, another man in a motor boat retrieves what is shot.

TWO-MAN LAYOUT BOAT ON LAKE EERIE
"I'll tell you what's religious about hunting," one Lake Eerie old-timer told me as he whittled away on a cedar decoy. "If you're out there in a layout and it starts to blow up good, you pray like hell!"

INDIAN DUCK HUNTER:
To the Montagnais-Naskapi (of Eastern Canada)–hunters on the barest subsistence level–the animals of the forest, the tundra, and the waters of the interior and coast exist in a specific relation. They have become objects of engorssing magico-religious activity, for to them, hunting is a holy occupation. —Frank Speck[4]

Patience

Stalking, tracking, racing, crouching, or crawling, the hunter proceeds forward, becoming a predator like a big cat or a wolf. But more often, the animals come to the waiting hunter, who uses concealment like a snapping turtle to avoid detection.

> *"You must learn to wait properly."*
> *"And how does one learn that? "*
> *"By letting go of yourself, leaving yourself and everything of yours behind you so decisively that nothing more is left of you but a purposeless tension . . . ."*

EUGENE HERRIGEL[5]

Driving

The individual hunter relies on concealment and stealth to get close enough for a killing shot. Quietness is of paramount value to this style of hunting.

There are forms of hunting, however, that date back centuries, where large numbers of people are enlisted to drive game toward hunters. In Europe, driven hunts are still conducted. Numerous beaters turn out, form lines, and walk through cover, making loud noises so as to drive game toward hunters who wait in concealment. The hunters must shoot over the heads of beats, or only at game that is overhead or passed through their ranks. With shooters shooting toward them and anxious animals racing back and forth, driven hunts can be both exciting and dangerous. In the south of Spain, it is customary for the drivers to come together to pray before commencing a monteria, or driven hunt. The following is a prayer that was given to me by a Spanish guide/outfitter, Francisco Rosich:

Royal Brotherhood of the Most Holy Virgin of the Head Savior of the Mountaineer

Lord who saves you, Virgin of the Head, Queen and Mother of mercy, from sunlit areas of Jandula, overseer of the formidable peaks.

Life, sweetness and hope that arise from the grandeur of your mountain altar, enclosed in the columns of rock and the sweet pine nuts of Tamujar and of Rosalejo, high above the plateau of the Sierra Madrona.

We call to you, Mistress of the stony and wild regions, we, the exiled children of Eve, that come to You, seeking your intangible light that illuminates the rocky cliffs.

We long for You, Patron Saint of the pathways and streams, coming before you with humility, with tears, with our humble offering, we come to the valley at your feet, asking for your presence to be with us in those valleys which lie from Estena to Bembezar, from Bullaque to Sardinia, from Jandula to Guadiana that are mosaics in the map of Spain.

And so, Mistress, guardian of your high sanctuary, wreathed and unique, we ask you to bless those lands that you watch over so clearly, sweet and protected from the harsh darkness of Alacondes and Contadero, until the bright smile of your benediction shines from Valdelagrana to El Socor.

Watch over us with your enduring eyes, so that the strength of your protection extends to the distant hills of Hornachuelos and the Sierra of the San Pedro, to the savage mountains of Madrid and Toledo, to the snows of the Pyrenees and Cantabria, where the people of strong resolve reside, worshipping the Holy Creation, as manifested through you from the sky above to the land below.

For while we may have been banished from the Garden of Eden, we can find forgiveness and enjoy the fruits of the Holy Fruit of Jesus through your blessings, Virgin saint.

Oh Divine Clemency! Oh Holiness! Oh always sweet Virgin Mary! To those of us who love the remote solitude of the wilds, please protect us with your warm cape, as we travel through the pure air of the mountains that bathe in the crowning light of your Sanctuary.

Pray for us, Sweet Mother of God, so that we may be worthy of receiving the guidance and protection of such previous honored gentlemen as Eustace the Roman, Herman the Gaul, and Hubert of Acquitaine, so that we may receive the safe passage and blessing of Jesus Christ.

Amen.

Long live the Virgin de Cabeza!

In old China the hunting rule was that the animals might be driven together by men to three corners of the horizon, but the fourth corner had to be an open space to give them a chance; God would inspire them to escape in the right direction if their time hadn't come. I read in the paper that the Swiss government has issued a similar rule.

MARIE-LOUISE VON FRANZ[6]

A TYPICAL "REHALA" (GROUP OF HUNTING DOGS) FOR "MONTERIA". c. 1936

"When one is hunting, the air has another, more exquisite feel as it glides over the skin or enters the lungs, the rocks acquire a more expressive physiognomy, and the vegetation becomes loaded with meaning. But all this is due to the fact that the hunter, while he advances or waits crouching, feels tied through the earth to the animal he pursues, whether the animal is in view, hidden, or absent . . ."

JOSE ORTEGA Y GASSET[7]

"A hunter should never let himself be deluded by pride or false sense of dominance. It is not through our power that we take life in nature; it is through the power of nature that life is given to us."

RICHARD NELSON[8]

Driven hunt-Manuel Benedito, painter. "The return from a Monteria", c. 1910 (Banco De Urquilo collection, Madrid)

The Dukes of Almazan at a Monteria, c.1934 (Cordoba, Analucia, Spain)

A Group of Hunters at a "Monteria", 1925 (Cordoba, Analucia, Spain)

CHAPTER 12

The Kill

Prayer for the Wildthings

Oh Great Spirit, give me guidance to take in all your wonderment.
Help me observe and embrace my role as a Bloodbrother to nature.
Teach me to use my gifts of reason and intellect to better connect with
the fruits of the earth. Inspire me to practice diligently so as to receive your
hoofed, furred, and feathered gifts of sustenance for my family, by killing
cleanly that which we can utilize and share with our neighbors.
Bless me with the rewards of full participation in your grand creation.
Make all our hunts safe, peaceful and complete.
Fill me, great father, with the Spirit of the Wild. Thank you for life.

TED NUGENT[1]

Some 40 million years ago a small animal that looked like a weasel, but had a tail as long as its entire body, walked the earth. Paleontologists named it *Miacis*. While small in stature, in evolutionary terms *Miacis* is enormously important, for it is considered the common ancestor of all carnivores, including the dog and the bear, even though it looked like neither.

As time passed, the dogs grew longer legs for speed, while the bears grew large bodies and became strong, some reaching prodigious proportions. Professor Valerius Geist has speculated that an abundant population of the giant Paleolithic cave bears, *Arctodus simus*, may have slowed the land bridge migration from Asia to North America.

Some have called the lion the king of beasts, but to many cultures, it is the bear that is the ruler of the animal kingdom. Odin, the supreme god of Norse mythology, is sometimes drawn as a bear. In Japan, the bear is associated with the goddess of compassion, Kwan-Yin. Bears that have a crescent-shaped white moon mark on their throat are said to be special allies of Kwan-Yin. Worshippers of Artemis, and her Roman counterpart, Diana, were called "she-bears," for both wore bearskins and were said to draw on the powers of bears to protect animals.

The earliest hero in Anglo-Saxton literature is Beowulf, a name derived from "bee-wolf," the name given to bears for their love of honey. The King Arthur legend is derived from the Celtic root "art," which means "bear." Some clans and families in many parts of the world even consider themselves descended from bears.

The apes resemble man more than any animal, but while chimpanzees do hunt like we do, they do not hunt men. There are seven species of bear. All can walk erect, adroitly use their paws, and show cleverness in thought and action. Among Plains Indians of the United States, people who have recurring dreams of bears are said to have a special gift for healing with herbs.

Bears and man occupy much the same niche in the food chain — both are omnivores — and they also eat each other. The fact that they have practiced mutual predation since the Paleolithic era may be one reason why reverence for the bear is so common in native customs, for as Dudley Young has written, "What is religious about hunting is that it leads us to remember and accept the violent nature of our condition, that every animal that eats will in turn one day be eaten. The hunt keeps us honest."[2]

According to religious historian Mircea Eliade, the bear is the principal archetypal symbol of the mythology of the hunt all around the world wherever he is found. Archery pioneer Fred Bear once said that hunting a grizzly or brown bear with a bow and arrow would "cleanse the soul." William Faulkner captured the haunting spirit of stalking a huge bear about as well as anyone when he wrote the following:

> It ran in his knowledge before he ever saw it. It loomed and towered in his dreams before he ever saw the unaxed woods where it left its crooked print, shaggy, tremendous, red-eyed, not malevolent but just big, too big for the dogs which tried to bay it, for the horses which tried to ride it down, for the men and the bullets they fired into it; too big for the very country which it was considering scope . . . not even a mortal beast, but an anachronism indomitable and invincible out of a dead time, a phantom, epitome, and apotheosis of the old wild life.[3]

Around the globe in Arctic regions, bear hunting is the most ritualized form of hunting among native people. Before the hunt begins, hunters pray, fast, undergo spiritual cleansing in saunas or sweat lodges, make offerings and conduct rituals. A new language is spoken, or no words are used at all. While the hunters are afield, women and children are supposed to be

If there is a sacred moment in the ethical pursuit of game, it is the moment you release the arrow or touch off the fatal shot.

Jim Postewitz[6]

＊┈━┽◈┾━┈＊

quiet. To carry on extramarital affairs during this time is believed to bring on ill fortune. This behavior not only aligns hunters with the gods in hopes of good luck, it also shows respect for the bear, whose spirit is the most powerful of all. The bear is said to be the mediator between man and the animals.

Wherever bears are found, native people conduct special rituals to honor the spirit of their slain brother, for many believe that if the bear is not shown proper respect, its spirit will return and wreak havoc on people's lives. Among the Kwakiutl Indians of British Columbia, when a hunter kills a bear, the hunter must follow a proper ritual to honor the soul of the bear. He begins by sitting on the ground on the right side of the bear. Then he says:

Thank you, friend, that you did not make me walk about in vain. Now you have come to take mercy on me so that I may obtain game, that I may inherit your power of getting easily with your hands the salmon that you catch.

Now I will press my right hand against your left hand [says the man as he takes hold of the left paw of the bear, and then continues].

O friend, now that we press together our working hands, that you may give over to me your power of getting everything easily with your hands, friend.[4]

Only after this prayer has been said, can the hunter begin skinning the bear.

The bear is a dominant force in the mythology and culture of Scandinavia, where Teutonic warriors once conducted berserker ceremonies to take on the spirit of an angry bear in war.

Often in bear cultures, a special feast is held to honor a slain bear. In the Finnish epic poem, *The Kalevala*, the hero, Vainamoinen, addresses a bear he has slain as if he is talking with the guest of honor at a banquet:

Where shall I take my guest, lead my golden one?

Shall I perhaps take him to the shed, put him in the hay barn?

In answer the people say, the handsome group spoke up:

"You will take our special guest yonder, lead our golden one under the splendid ridge-pole, under the lovely roof. There food has been prepared, drinks got ready, all the floor-boards cleaned, the floors swept; all the women dressed in fresh clothes with pretty head ornaments, in white clothes.[5]

All around the northern hemisphere, among the native traditions — Saami, the Ainu, the Inuit, the northern Norwegians, Finns and Swedes, Native Indian tribes of the United States and Canada, and all the various tribes of Russia, Mongolia and Siberia — hunting is the driving spirit of culture. While many animals and fish have economic importance and food value, the bear is generally the most sacred of all the animals. He is generally seen as all-seeing and all-knowing, has a soul like a man, and is the intermediary between man and all other animals.

Among the Saami, the bear hunt was presided over by the god *Leib-olma*i or Alder Man. While Bears were not seen as gods to worship, they were said to possess supernatural powers. To protect themselves from *Rachemacht*, or revenge of the bear, women chewed the bark of the alder tree and spit it on themselves and hunters who returned from a successful hunt. As an extra precaution, the hunters also had to enter the *kota*, or hut, through a rear door, a holy door, to neutralize the spirit of the bear and keep it away, if it was offended in any way.

Once the bear was killed, all of its bones were carefully buried in a grave, often in the same pattern as the skeleton of the bear. This place was not a holy place, but was treated just like a human grave. Saami also showed respect for spirits of other animals killed by leaving their antlers and bones at the place where the animals died.

The Moment of Truth

Up until a certain moment in the hunt, the emotional chemistry between man and nature, especially man and animals, is the same whether hunting with a 35mm Nikon camera, a powerful pair of Bushnell binoculars, or a Remington shotgun. Man and beast are engaged in a game of proximity.

Raising a lethal weapon and taking aim changes the rules of the game, separating hunting from shooting at targets, or taking pictures. Charged with awareness that this "target" has a mind of its own, emotional intensity roars into overdrive. Stalking is no longer a concern. This is the moment of truth. Normally steady hands and knees tremble like a willow sapling in a wind. Tears well up in the eyes. The hunter may want to cough, because the mouth and throat are dry, but can't. He or she may suddenly need to pee, but can't. Time stands still. Normal breathing sounds as loud as a winter

windstorm. The hunted and hunter are both in the "magic zone" of life and death and the hunter's challenge now is to contain all that emotion into transfer attention to a mechanical device — gun, bow, slingshot — and perform a task the way it has been done countless times at the practice range, and which suddenly seems so far removed. "Buck fever" never really goes away. A hunter just learns to manage it better with time.

With an awareness that he intends to take the life of a beautiful, perhaps even majestic creature, the hunter must decide, sometimes in a split second, if the check-list of criteria are all okay — species and sex of the animal, safety of the shot, distance to the animal, speed of the game, wind that could influence accuracy or bring a telltale scent, recovery potential, angle of the shot and its trajectory through the air and into the animal. If all systems are "go," then with the hunter's prayer in mind ("If I shoot, God, let me miss clean, or let me kill clean and recover the animal"), the hunter steps out from all the other nature lovers and performs a lethal act.

The Kill

Just a moment ago it was a 12-pound Canada goose, rushing along on the wind at 40 miles an hour, and then, as if touched by an invisible wand, it fell to earth like a rock. With small game, the moment of death is almost always seen. With larger animals, death may come quietly, without a witness. Shot with a bow and arrow or a bullet through lungs and heart, a deer will travel usually less than 100 yards, then lay down and die by bleeding to death in less

---

The hunt is not something which happens to the animal by chance: rather in the instinctive depths of his nature he has already foreseen the hunter.

JOSE ORTEGA Y GASSET[7]

than a minute. Shock curbs pain, as anyone who has ever been seriously wounded knows. There have been many accounts of a deer being shot by a sharp broadhead, the arrow passing entirely through the body, the deer flinching as if bitten by a fly, and then resuming feeding. Moments later, it slumps to the ground and dies. The swifter the death, the better. Only a sadist enjoys suffering, and as Erich Fromm has observed, the normal, ethical hunter is not a sadist.[8] Rather, he or she is a lover. In embracing the love-death dance of life, the hunter reaches a depth of nature kinship that is hard to approximate by those who remain witnesses, rather than participants, in the food chain.

Coming upon the still-warm animal, the hunter's heart is touched. Tears may come to eyes: a rare mixture of sadness, love and excitement. Kahlil Gibran captures this moment well:

> When you kill a beast say to him in your heart,
>
> "By the same power that slays you, I too am slain; and I too shall be consumed.
>
> For the law that delivered you into my hand shall deliver me into a mightier hand.
>
> Your blood and my blood is naught but the sap that feeds the tree of heaven."[9]

It is in this moment of truth that many hunters find prayers coming to their lips without thought or planning; when love flows from the heart like water from an artesian spring guided by the religious instinct that Carl Jung

PETROGLYPH OF SHEEP WITH TWO ARROWS IN IT

and Marie-Louise von Franz spoke of. A minister once told me that he had felt the presence of God most strongly in his life when his children were born and when he killed his first deer.

Veteran film and television actor Marshall Teague shares a prayer he always says when his gun or bow finds success: "Lord, bless this noble creature that has given his time and spirit to engage in the chase. Permit him green pastures to graze, thick forests to roam, and take his heart and soul into your blessed hands." Marshall adds that if he misses and the animal gets away, thanks should also be given, for life should never be taken for granted.

Winged boy of the clear-voiced Cyprian goddess. Thou that dwellest in Helliconian Thespiae by the flowery garden of Narcissus, graciously accept the gift that Hadrian gives you, the spoils of the bear. He slew it with his own hand, striking it from horseback. Do thou in return temporarily breathe grace upon him from heavenly Aphrodite.

HADRIAN, ROMAN EMPEROR, AD 117-138
(ON A STONE FOUND AT THESPIAE IN CENTRAL GREECE)

*"I do not kill with my gun; he who kills with his gun
has forgotten the face of his father.
I kill with my heart."*

STEPHEN KING[10]

CHAPTER 13

Celebrating Success

*. . . it is virtually a standard rule among hunters that they should never mock
or otherwise insult any wild creature whose life they have brought to an end.
Their rationalization, if they do rationalize about it, is that
such disrespect will offend the spirits that control game supply.*

CARLETON COON[1]

lood is what makes us alive, or dead. Blood is associated with maturity, with killing to eat or to defend oneself and community, and with the onset of menstruation. Blood signals the mystery of life and death. Getting one's hands bloody enables one to assume responsibility for being a part of the food chain, making our species honest, as well as affecting ecological balance.

"Firsts" are benchmarks of life. The first kill of a hunter is a milestone. Seeing, firsthand, the results of your own hunting, as you regard an animal that minutes before was filled with life, is a moment most hunters will never forget. "First blood" is a giant step toward completion, whenever it comes.

In 1950, when he was 10 years old, a family friend, B.J. Armistead Sr., invited George P. Mann to go deer hunting at the Armistead family homestead in West Alabama. Some four decades later, Mann recalls that he was, "so excited I couldn't sleep for over a month until the day arrived." Luck was with Mann, and on his first outing he killed a buck with four-inch spikes. That evening, back at the lodge, Armistead had young George stand up before everyone, and dipping his finger into the deer's blood, he painted smears onto Mann's face, initiating him into the society of hunters in a ceremony that supposedly began centuries before in Europe. We mark important passages of life by ceremonies and rituals to formally acknowledge a person's accomplishments and to express social approval and praise. That blooding ceremony has had a lifelong effect on Mann.

As Mann grew older, his love for hunting also grew, as did his success in the metal fabricating industry. Around his home in Opelika, Alabama, there were no deer, so in 1965, with the support of the Alabama Fish and Game Department, Mann initiated a trapping and stocking program to bring deer into Lee County. They began with 13 the first year. By

BLOODING CEREMONY:
George P. Mann's conducts blooding for a successful "first deer" hunter.

improving the habitat, the herd began to grow, and record-size bucks began to be taken. Feeling so strongly about taking his first deer, and its impact on his life as a hunter and conservationist, George Mann set aside a tract of several hundred acres of his personal land specifically for people to take their first deer. As the years passed, he also introduced wild turkeys. As of 1999, more than 224 hunters have killed their first deer on Mann's property. For each, George conducts the blooding ceremony, just as Armistead did for him. A special high point of his initiation program came when he repaid B.J. Armistead for initiating him into hunting, by guiding Armistead, at age 86, on his first successful wild boar hunt.

His years of hunting and being the initiator of so many hunters moved Mann to make his next step in honoring the heritage of hunting. In the spring of 1999, on the outskirts of Opelika, Alabama, he opened a 34,000-square-foot outdoor education center, the Mann Museum and Outdoors, situated on a 10-acre tract of land set aside as a nature preserve. With exhibits designed by Henry Inchumuk, the museum contains numerous mounted fish and animals, along with fossil relics, and is already a popular attraction for school groups and tourists.

"Blooding" is an initiation ritual performed for first kills worldwide. In George Butler's 1989 feature length docudrama film, *In the Blood*, which retraces Theodore Roosevelt's 1909 African safari with Theodore Roosevelt IV and V, professional hunter Robin Hurt performs a blooding ceremony on Tyssen Butler, who has taken his first big game animal, a cape buffalo, using Roosevelt's famous Holland and Holland rifle.

A DRIVEN HUNT AND CONCLUDING "THANKSGIVING" CEREMONY IN GERMANY:
These photos of a driven hunt in Germany were taken in 1953. The hunt took place on what is today the Munich International Airport. According to photographer–writer Wolfgang Alexander Bajohr, the bag on this day's hunt was: 160 hares, 5 ducks, 1 fox and one other bird. At the conclusion of the hunt, all the animals are laid out in a specific format, torches are lighted and hunters with horns stand at each of the four corners and blow a thanksgiving salute.

Standing over the fallen animal, they talk about emotions — excitement, fear and sadness at the death of a majestic animal. Then, as the African guides begin to cut open the animal, Hurt says, "Tyssen, this is the most important part. Do you know what you've done? You've just taken your first animal. That's a special moment."

Hurt then dips his hand into the buffalo's blood, takes Tyssen by the shoulder, and directs him to face toward the horizon, looking into the sun.

"Let's look over there, into the horizon," Hurt says. "This is where this buffalo has lived all his life. Beautiful piece of country."

After a nostalgic pause, Hurt turns to Tyssen and paints blood across the boy's forehead and cheeks as two African trackers excitedly warble a high-pitched tremolo of praise. When he is finished, Hurt says, "Congratulations."

The trackers step forward and paint Tyssen's face, and hearty handshakes are exchanged by all. Tyssen has just joined the membership of big game hunters, a social group as old as man himself, with a ceremony perhaps nearly as old.

Scottish hunting guide Michael Roberts relates that in Poland some hunting guides conduct blooding rites to make the cross of Saint Hubert in blood on the hunter's face. The hunter kneels beside the animal. The guide dips his knife in the blood of the wound then presses the knife blade vertically on one cheek, and then horizontally to make a cross. This is repeated on the other cheek, and finally on the forehead. Some guides make the cross just on the hunter's forehead. When this is done, the guide shakes the hunter's hand and stands up.

Healing

The feature film *The Deer Hunter* chronicles the impact of post-traumatic stress syndrome on a man, poisoning his hunting, as well as his emotional life. Contrarily, photojournalist Cork Graham recounts a time when hunting helped him heal the wounds of war:

Moose Hunt, Healing Heart

Crowberries in Alaska always taste best during moose season. Sarah Seesfar calls me over to enjoy the bounty of fall that stretches down to the flat spruce-covered bog. I am more interested in seeing if Sarah can, as she claims, call a moose to her rifle like her ancestors. It's a feat I've heard my Scottish ancestors could do with red deer. Sarah is half Athabascan, and her attractive, thick, long black braid makes her appear as though she just stepped out of an illustration for a collection of the poems of Robert Service.

Suddenly, Sarah lifts her hand, palm open. I halt. She kneels, I kneel. Freezing water seeps through my army surplus pants. My rifle, a bolt action .280 Remington, is to my shoulder like lightning, more out of habit than desire, as memories of the Central American rain forest war sweep through my mind, reminding me of scars I carry.

I look over at Sarah. She has shaded her eyes with her hand and stares intently into a thicket of spruce surrounded by alders, far down on the other side of the flat. Quickly, Sarah stands and waves me to follow her in a mad scramble down the hill and into the trees.

Entering the first stand, we pass into a circle of open grass. A sense of peace overtakes me, much like an empty kirk in the afternoon. Sarah kneels again, and I follow.

This time she mumbles. It's her language, not mine, but I get the sense that she is praying for all of us: Sarah and me and the moose she hopes to kill. I might have said 'I am to kill,' too, but my heart is not in it, even though I can think of nothing tastier than lightly grilled moose round steak. I'm more taken by the daydream-inducing beauty of the spruce and muskeg, and the crisp break from the week's rains.

"Here he comes," Sarah startles me. I see no movement.

She answers my disbelief with an index finger to her lips. Again she mumbles in prayer, in a language I wish I could speak, much like I wish I could speak Scots-Gaelic as fluently as my father could.

A long while passes. Or, so it seems. More so because of the way my mind wanders. At once I'm thrown back into El Salvador, waste deep in a mangrove swamp, unsuccessfully attempting to keep a good friend from bleeding to death by sucking a chest wound, and then just as suddenly in a firefight shooting an FMLN guerrilla as he charges me with a raised machete. He falls like a wet sheet. There is no drama in my memory, just sadness and a feeling that I have left a part of myself in a tropical swamp.

The pressure of a hand on my shoulder brings me back to Alaska and Sarah's smile. It was Sarah's own spiritual teacher who suggested she hunt to deal with the darkness of her sexual abuse and guilt, and her own resulting post-traumatic stress. Sarah had told me how, at first, as she had paid homage to the animal she killed through prayer and rejoiced in the food that the animal's body would give her, she transferred the release of guilt of killing to the guilt she felt from her childhood experience. Continuing to hunt throughout the rest of her life, she never again felt the same type of guilt or lack of love for herself

that so many times brought her close to suicide.

The unmistakable clatter of antler against branches draws me to stare at the large behemoth suddenly before us, only 10 feet away.

"Take your time," Sarah whispers. I shake my head. Somehow proximity of the spike moose and the big black eyes that stare down at me as though I were a child character in Doctor Doolittle makes me falter as I bring the rifle to my shoulder. The moose is so close that I can't even use the scope on my rifle that's set to its lowest power of three.

Hoarsely, I whisper back, "You take him."

She glares back at me. "Don't disrespect us all by turning down this offering."

I put my cheek back against the stock, and squeeze the trigger, breaking the silence. Dropping to the muskeg, but with the smallest of sound, the moose lays on its side. I am stunned. Not only by the size of the animal that must now be butchered, but by the ease with which this kill has happened.

Sarah takes my hand and touches it to the blood that flows from an initial burst to a barely noticeable leak, and wipes my cheeks with the warm blood. She then asks me to smear the blood on her cheeks, too. In a daze, I do so. And then she prays. I look back out onto the bog and am reminded of Scotland and the peace my Pict and Gaelic ancestors must have felt before the English came.

I want to join in, but again, I don't know the words. This time, though, it doesn't seem to matter, because I feel the words come to me. "Thank you, oh great moose. . . Thank you for all you offer."

Suddenly, a low whimpering catches my attention. I am caught by surprise because I realize that the sobbing is not Sarah's, but mine. Tears stream down my face and try that I may, I can't hold them back, as they release the sudden stabbing in my heart.

My thoughts jump to the realization that when I've been angry lately, the feeling of anger was not only the result of whatever experience may have naturally come up, but also the extra impact of never before having dealt with the emotions resulting from my experiences as a media member in the Central American war. I am suddenly aware of how this kill and the tears that I feel for this moose are not only for the moose, but also for those I killed in combat. Meditating more, I tell myself, as Sarah told me to do, that the two are one, and the tears I wash with now are in thanks to the moose and to those who died so that I may now live.

From under a cut she makes in the moose's hide, Sarah draws a piece of dark, red, meat. The chuck looks like a ruby. It bears no resemblance to the meat I've bought so many times in the supermarket, which so often looks like it has been lightly sprayed with gray paint.

I take the warm bloody flesh in my mouth and hold it. I chew, amazed that there is no urge to vomit or spit. I savor the taste that seems to calm my breathing and release the pain in my heart. Sarah smiles at me, and says, "Take of your holy offering. Realize that today, as every day from now on, is a new day and that your life is as precious as was this one's who feeds you now. Don't waste it."

Gary Snyder's Grace

We venerate the Three Treasures (teachers, the wild and friends)
And we are thankful for this meal,
The work of many people,
And the sharing of other forms of life.

GARY SNYDER[2]

Food

During the past century, breeding and feeding practices [have] increased the proportion of fat . . . in response to consumer demand for ever-more-tender meat. The marbling of muscle and thick layers of insulating fat found in supermarket meat shows the results of these efforts. Indeed, the carcasses of today's domesticated animals are 25 to 30 percent fat, while a survey of forty-three different species of wild game animals from three continents has revealed an average fat content of only 4.3 percent.

S.B Eaton, M. Shostak
and M. Konner[3]

Membership

Initiation means joining something new. For some hunters the first kill means a step toward adulthood. With it comes membership in special societies. Today's hunting clubs are the modern descendants of yesterday's hunting clans.

A hunting club is more than a place to sleep, eat, drink and play cards. At their best, they are custodians of magic, mystery, spirit and service; preserving a legacy that traces back to the secret hunting societies of the Paleolithic.

Pte Mouillee Hunt Club on Lake Erie, circa 1880, was at one time one of the most well known and respected waterfowl hunting clubs in the United States. Today the area is a public hunting refuge.

CHAPTER 14

Service

*If sentimentalists were right, hunting would develop
in man a cruelty of character. But I have found that
it inculcates patience, demands discipline and iron nerve,
and develops a serenity of spirit that makes
for a long life and a long love of life.*

ARCHIBALD RUTLEDGE[1]

Primal instincts, unrestrained, are ripe to commit deadly sins. There is a dark shadow in the mastery of hunting that must be addressed. Would not the veteran hunter, who has mastered the skills of taking game, be prone to decimate wildlife?

While the skills may be there, research shows that just the opposite is true. When professors Robert Jackson and Robert Norton of the University of Wisconsin–LaCrosse interviewed more than 1,000 hunters, they identified a consistent pattern of hunter behavior change.[2] Neophytes start out as shooters, testing out their marksmanship. As they become proficient shots, their goal changes from hitting game to bagging a limit. As their competency increases, their interests shift to

trophies, and patience grows. As this stage is mastered, hunters often shift to more primitive technologies, to increase the challenge. Ultimately, those hunters who stick with it become sportsmen — experts capable of taking game when others don't. But, they may restrict their methods or acceptable bag limits even further, such as shooting only drake mallards or whitetail bucks with 10 points or more. Accepting self-imposed restrictions, they find that the experience of hunting is now so deep and profound that being afield, regardless of whether a shot is fired or not, is enormously rewarding in itself. Veteran Alaskan guide and author Bob Robb shares a tale of an encounter with a blacktail buck that illustrates the heart of a seasoned sportsman:

The Gorge

"This is crazy," I thought as I leaned my sweat-soaked back against the trunk of an ancient oak. Its shade seemed a blessing. The mercury on my tiny belt thermometer was nearly off the scale at 105 sizzling degrees. I closed my eyes and wondered why I still hunted deer in August in southern California's early coastal zone. Actually, I knew why. Nobody else would probably be willing to do this, especially in this heat.

It was a two-mile hike down an old Forest Service road just to get to the edge of this God-forsaken canyon, where the walls fell away so steep that a mountain goat might have trouble not slipping. This particular canyon was known for mosquitoes, ticks, big black flies, and the Mojave green, a rattlesnake that grows over six feet long and has an attitude. From the shade of this oak, I could see a small, level area, a quarter of a mile below: a flat marked by oaks loaded with acorns and a tiny seep, the only source of water for miles.

One didn't hunt this gorge for smaller bucks. This was where you hunted the oldest and wisest of the blacktails, bucks that had survived the masses who drove the Forest Service roads in their 4x4s and called themselves hunters.

I took a siesta, as I assumed the deer also would. When I awoke, the sun was down-sliding, although the thermometer was still 100 plus, too hot even for the mosquitoes. The heat reminded me of those stories my mother used to tell me about hell when I got a bit out of line.

I saw the first deer of the day a little after five. It was a big, mature forked-horn buck — what my father had called a Pacific buck — with medium-heavy antlers and no eyeguards. He was about a half-mile away, slowly moving toward the oaks. Soon a doe and a yearling joined him, their ears constantly flapping at the black flies.

My senses went on the alert. I couldn't see

him yet, but I just knew there was a good buck down there. And then he appeared, a tan ghost that materialized seemingly from thin air. He stepped halfway out of a patch of dark shade, head erect for a moment, before slipping into the thick manzanita. His antlers were wider than his ears, and at least twice as tall. The bases were thick, and I could see three points on one side and four on the other. He was the biggest blacktail buck I had ever seen.

For the first time since taking up my glassing position, I picked up my rifle. This was a very special gun. It had belonged to my father, who had purchased it back in the last 1940s for $250 — a lot of money back then for a man of modest means just back from the war. A Model 70 Winchester chambered in .270. The battered stock, worn leather sling, and barrel rubbed almost white in places spoke of the countless days and hours he had spent hunting to help feed the family, as well as for sport. He had taken over 40 bucks with this gun.

I tried to read the buck's mind. What would he do? He continued toward the oak grove. There was a small opening coming up in his path. I considered rolling prone and trying for a shot. The rifle could do it, but I quickly discarded the idea. This was an animal to be respected. He deserved a well-placed shot at close range.

I found a narrow trail, more of a tunnel through heavy brush, which ran behind the rise that paralleled his projected path. I took a gamble. A shift in the wind, a change in the thermals, a little slip on the loose shale or the snap of a tinder-dry twig, and he would only be a memory. The going was slow for an adrenaline-charged man. I never noticed the heat, the sweat or the flies.

I finally found an opening. No deer. My shirt was soaked with sweat and dust had formed a gritty film all over me. I belly-up crawled another 40 yards and peaked over the ridge. Almost immediately I saw him, a hundred yards off. His tall antlers looked awesome.

Suddenly, the buck snapped his head to attention and, body rigid, stared straight at me. I could have sworn that I hadn't made a sound. He stared at me for a full minute — a lifetime — then he flicked his ears and the tension left his eyes. He continued his slow, careful approach to the flat. Within minutes (or was it hours?), he was 50 yards off. I marveled at his antlers. Magnificent.

I waited for the deer to turn his head away from my general direction. When he did, I slowly raised the rifle to my shoulder. The heat and tension turned my hands into a sweaty mess. My heart was doing its best to beat its way out of my chest as the crosshairs found his vital area just behind the front shoulder.

I slid my finger over the trigger and drew a short breath. I knew what I must do.

"Bang," I whispered.

Slowly lowering the rifle, I stood. The buck snorted and took a couple of short steps that looked like a hyperactive eight-year-old on a pogo stick. He snapped his head in my direction, saw that I was a man, and was off like a shot, disappearing into a small oak grove. A moment later he paused on the ridgeline, a ghost-like silhouette of tan and brown against the deepening colors of twilight, before trotting over the rim.

I stared at the spot for some time, hands shaking lightly, sweat dripping, my heart beating faster than ever. I closed my eyes. The buck had been mine. I had suffered for hours for just such an opportunity, yet when the moment of truth was there, I had elected not to squeeze the trigger. It felt right. As I replayed the scene over and over in my mind, savoring every detail, it came to me. When I had first come on the canyon, slipping down the shale, the thought crossed my mind that I was treading on ground no man had ever tread on before.

Then, I found an ancient obsidian arrowhead. The find was both exciting and disappointing. The Indians of Ventura County used a term "Father of Many Bucktails" in their hunting rituals, believing that such a great buck possessed powerful medicine. His well-being was vital to the continued health of the herd. While they would vigorously hunt other animals, to kill this great deer was to place a curse on their primary meat source.

As I drove back down the mountain that night under the shining summer moon, I felt satisfied that this had been more than just a successful hunting trip.

A hero doesn't just accomplish something and rest on his or her laurels. If they do, then their valued status quickly declines and people see them as egotistical, perhaps even greedy and vain. Part of the responsibility for receiving the community's honor of being a hero is to perform acts of service, heroic acts made possible by hero status. In the case of hunters, the service is to both man and nature.

One could argue that the conservation efforts of hunters are simply compensatory to work off guilt associated with killing animals. That would be a naive assumption, for it fails to acknowledge the sense of love and respect for nature that arises from surrendering to the spirit of the hunt. The sentiment of the spirit of the hunt that moves hunters to community service is ultimately reverence and compassion, not the seeking of redemption.

The conservation movement is one of the most significant political movements of the 20th century. Most people associated its birth with passionate hunter Theodore Roosevelt. What far too few people know is that the seed of the conservation movement originated with one of Roosevelt's closest friends, Gifford Pinchot, in an experience that psychologists would describe as an adamic ecstacy — a moment of brilliant clarity following an extended period of depression and confusion.

The Birth of the Conservation Movement

On a foggy February morning in 1905, Gifford Pinchot, avid outdoorsman and chief forester for the U.S. government, rode his horse, Jim, through Rock Creek Park in Washington, D.C. Pinchot was deeply depressed. His close friend President Theodore Roosevelt had asked him to come up with a unifying policy to guide and manage all the natural resources of the country. A forester trained in the best schools of America and Europe, Pinchot

GIFFORD PINCHOT
Theodore Roosevelt is credited with launching the conservation movement, but in his autobiography, he corrected that statement, saying, "... Gifford Pinchot is the man to whom the nation owes most for what has been accomplished as regards the preservation of the natural resources of the country." 3

Ducks Unlimited Marsh Conservation sign

understood the scientific aspects of resource management, but the thought of one theme to encompass all forests, wildlife, minerals, waterways, fisheries, range lands and parks, seemed beyond reach. In the middle of a fog of confusion, suddenly he slipped into a reverie where he found himself looking down what appeared to be a long tube. At the other end appeared a lush tract of forest in India, in lands called Conservancies that were managed for the public good. As he recognized the land in his vision, the words, "The greatest good for the greatest number for the longest time," flashed into his mind.

Pinchot took his revelation to a close group of friends, to help him make sense of it as he prepared to share his thoughts with President Roosevelt. In his autobiography, *Breaking New Ground*, Pinchot gives credit to W.J. McGee, who was then head of the Bureau of Soils, for helping him realize the full ramifications of his insight for charting the future of natural resource policy. McGee coined the word "Conservation" and refined the definition as, "The wise use of natural resources for the greatest number of people for the longest time."[4] Thus was launched the Conservation Movement, which Roosevelt later said was the most important contribution of his administration.

During the seven-and-one-half years of his presidency, aided by Pinchot, Theodore Roosevelt was responsible for establishing five national parks (Crater Lake in Oregon, Wind Cave in South Dakota, Platte in Oklahoma, Sully Hill in North Dakota, and Mesa Verde in Colorado); four big game refuges and 52 bird sanctuaries; the first game laws in Alaska; the buffalo herd in Yellowstone National Park; the National Monuments Act resulting in preserving Muir Woods, Pinnacles, and Mount Olympus National Monuments; the National Bison Range in Montana; and millions of acres of National Forest lands. He also held in 1908 the first White House Conference of Governors on Conservation, which

Conserving and Restoring Habitat

Waterfowl of all types, fish, and the entire food chain around them are dependent upon unpolluted wetlands. The United States as a whole has lost more than 50 percent of its original 220 million acres of wetlands, and the loss continues at roughly 170,000 acres a year. Some states, such as California, have lost more than 90 percent of their original wetlands. Only by aggressive action, largely from hunters' organizations, has it been possible to establish a stable population of waterfowl. Ducks Unlimited (DU) is the world's largest, privately funded conservation organization. Founded in 1937, DU has raised more than $1 billion for preserving, restoring and conserving wetlands and the wildlife that lives there. Out of every dollar taken in, 79 percent goes directly for habitat conservation programs.

DU is responsible for the conservation of nearly 9 million acres of wetlands in Canada, the United States and Mexico, as well as for placing millions more under conservation easements that restrict use in order to preserve wildlife habitat. More than 900 wildlife species can be found in DU projects, including 160 that are threatened or endangered.

led to the Report of the National Conservation Commission, an assessment of the state of the nation's natural resources, which Roosevelt asserted was "one of the most fundamentally important documents ever laid before the American people."

Giving Something Back

In the 20th century, the ancient hunting society has grown. Millions of hunters have banded together in organizations — such as Ducks Unlimited, Safari Club, Rocky Mountain Elk Foundation, the National Wildlife Turkey Federation, Foundation for North American Wild Sheep, Quail Unlimited, Pheasants Forever, Mule Deer Foundation, etc. as well as their counterparts abroad such as the Federation of Hunters Associations of Europe — to expedite the work of conserving wildlife. The success of their efforts is one of the great, largely unrecognized, stories of modern conservation. A brief overview illustrates why hunters remain heroes.

Conservation

Daily we hear stories about endangered species and extinctions. One estimate is that 25 percent of the mammals on the earth are endangered, with more than 1000 species of plants and animals facing extinction each year. The automatic assumption in the minds of many people is that hunters are a primary cause. Nothing could be further from the truth. Some extinction takes place as part of evolution and cannot be

SNOW GEESE IN WETLAND:
The United States has lost more than 50 percent of its original wetlands, which are the primary habitat for most all waterfowl. When one sees flocks like this, it's hard to imagine what it must have been like when there was twice as much wetlands.

stopped. When species have become threatened by loss of habitat, poaching or uncontrolled market harvesting, hunters have shown they will lead the fight to conserve wildlife.

In the United States many of the most popular game animals are more abundant than when Theodore Roosevelt was president, and the primary reason is hunter support of conservation and restoration work. The following is a synopsis of some of the success stories.

Wild Turkey — Following the Great Depression, when wild turkeys had been decimated by habitat loss, market hunting, and subsistence hunting, there were only about 30,000 wild turkeys left in the United States. Today, thanks to efforts led by the National Wild Turkey Federation, which has raised more than $90 million for turkey conservation in its first 25 years of existence, the population of wild turkeys numbers over 4.5 million, and wild turkeys can be found in every state except Alaska.

Canada Goose — In the 1940s the Canada goose population had dropped to slightly more than 1 million. At the end of the 20th century, it is beyond 2.5 million and growing. Some states now hold special seasons for nonmigratory populations that have fully adapted to living in modern urbanized areas, for they have become so common as to endanger airplane traffic and pollute small bodies of water, creating a health hazard.

Elk — Before European settlement, elk were found throughout North America in all areas but the modern states of Alaska and Florida. The herd was estimated at 10 million. By 1907, only approximately 41,000 were left in the wild. Again, market hunting and loss of habitat were key factors in the elk's decline. Today, there are more than 1 million elk and the herd is growing. A subspecies, the tule elk, found only in California wetlands, once dwindled to two in the wild. The tule elk has been saved and the herd numbers 3,000 and growing, which permits limited hunting.

Whitetail deer — There are probably more whitetail deer alive today than ever before, as this species has easily adapted to living in proximity with people. After decades of intense market hunting, in 1900 the U.S. population numbered approximately 500,000. Today it approaches 30 million.

Pronghorn antelope — In 1943, the antelope population of the United States was estimated at 12,000. Today, it is past 1 million and growing.

Wild Sheep — One hundred thousand years ago, Asian wild sheep migrated across the land bridge to North America. They settled into two large ice-free regions that today are roughly the Alaska-Yukon Territory and the American Southwest.

When the Mayflower landed, there were an estimated 1.5 to 2 million bighorn sheep in North America. The impact of modern society has been hard on these majestic creatures. Wild sheep of North America were hit hard by imported diseases from domestic sheep, competition for forage with domestic herds, and overhunting, especially market hunting. Unlike deer and elk, this is an animal that does not easily adapt to cohabitation with man. The bighorn population in the United States today is estimated at 43,000, and there are 72,000 snow white Dall sheep in Alaska.

Taking the lead in bighorn restoration has been the Foundation for North American Wild Sheep (FNAWS), founded in 1977. In its first 20 years of existence, FNAWS has raised nearly $15 million for projects underway through Mexico, Canada and the United States involving habitat protection and restoration of sheep herds.

One area where FNAWS has made a very significant impact is in the Hell's Canyon area of Washington-Idaho-Oregon, the largest intact tract of sheep habitat remaining in the United States. Covering more than 1 million acres, the area was devoid of bighorn sheep by 1945. Today, there are more than 700 wild sheep roaming this beautiful wilderness area, thanks to breeding stock transplanted from Canadian herds.

If you asked sheep hunters why they hunt bighorns, none of them could honestly say for food. Modern hunting is heavily regulated, with permits awarded only through lottery drawings. For many sheep hunters, getting drawn for a chance to hunt bighorns is a once in a lifetime matter.

African Elephant — As the largest land animals, elephants have long been prized for their ivory, which has driven down their numbers severely. In 1979, it is estimated the wild herd was 1.3 million. By 1989, it was sliced in half to 600,000. To curb the decline, importation of ivory was banned, and some countries forbade sport hunting for elephants. In places where hunting has been banned, elephant populations have plummeted even more. A case in point is Kenya, which banned elephant hunting in 1977. Poachers subsequently butchered the herds, as supervision of the animals also declined with the loss of revenue from hunting. In less than two decades, Kenya's elephant herd went from 150,000 to less than 6,000.

CELEBRATION OF A SUCCESSFUL ELEPHANT HUNT IN OMO, ETHIOPIA, IN 1993:
When an elephant is killed, people adorn themselves with a white ash made from burned elephant dung, and dance long into the night. Most of the dance is a recreation of the hunt.

Botswana, in contrast, has permitted big game hunting, and in the same period of time, their elephant herd has quadrupled. The key here is that hunters pump considerable money into the local economy, which increases the value of the animals to local natives, provides jobs and fresh meat for many, and supports wildlife research and law enforcement. It is estimated that hunters spend $35 million to $65 million dollars a year on African elephant hunting safaris. The white rhino in South Africa has similarly increased in numbers, thanks to hunter dollars.

"Make the game animals valuable, and the people will become stewards," asserts renowned African guide Robin Hurt. Experience all around the world supports his words.

— ᙓᛞᙓ —

Father guide my hands and heart so that no part of the animal will be wasted.

STEPHEN KING[5]

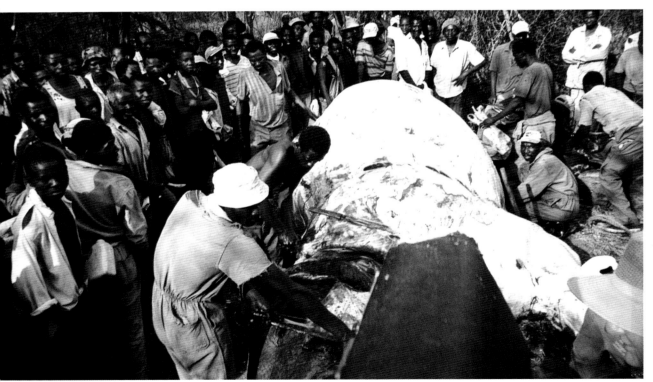

An entire village in Zimbabwe turns out *for their share of the meat of an elephant taken in a hunt associated with the CAMPFIRE program. In the Chobe Enclave in Botswana, twelve elephants may be shot every year, the meat shared among five nearby villages. The local people receive 20,000 pula per animal and nearly one million U.S. dollars for the concession. This is a program similar to the CAMPFIRE program.*

The Sacred Art of Hunting

Environmental Education

For many people today, the closest that they come to another species of animal is the "mouse" for their computer. And when we do go on vacation, what do we do? Studies have shown that the average visitor to a U.S. National Park spends six hours or less in the park, and that most of this time is spent in the car, at the rest room, and in the gift shop or restaurant. The average park visitor seldom goes more than 50 feet from the car to explore the park itself.

Since the earliest days of hunting, one of the responsibilities of hunters has been to bring the spirit of the wild into the community through stories. Yes, environmental education needs to teach vocabulary, scientific concepts and principles, and natural resource

Food

Hunters have always provided for the community's needs. Their traditional cultural role is to harvest wild meat and bring it back home to feed people. Carrying on the tradition, many people hold wild game dinners at season's end, celebrating the past season. This becomes an annual ritual, which helps keep strong ties to the original spirit of hunting. Some of these wild feasts are held at churches, serving as fund-raisers for church programs, serving as yet another example of the natural ties of hunting and charity where hunters act as heroes.

There is a growing movement among hunters in the United States to share some of the wild bounty with the poor and needy. Beginning in the 1970s, programs such as Hunters for the Hungry and Sportsman Against Hunger have grown rapidly throughout the United States. In 1998, Sportsmen Against Hunger, a project of Safari Club International, working in cooperation with the Salvation Army and other charitable and relief organizations, donated wild game meat that produced more than 4 million meals for

FROZEN WILD MEAT DONATED TO FEED THE POOR.

the poor and victims of natural disasters.

Addressing the spirit of service that is behind the Sportsmen Against Hunger program are two men world renown for service: Generals Norman Schwarzkopf and Chuck Yeager.

As a hunter, I gladly endorse the Sportsmen Against Hunger Program. We can all afford to share the fruits of our good fortune with our fellow men.
—CHARLES YEAGER,
BRIGADIER GENERAL, USAF RET.

We continue to be Sportsmen Against Hunger and donate our game to the homeless and the shelterless so that we can feed them. There's no end of things that everyone of you can do out there to show middle America that just because we hunt and fish does not mean that we are not contributing members of society... We care about our country and we're willing to contribute to our country.
—GENERAL NORMAN SCHWARZKOPF
(1996 speech to Safari Club International)

management theory. We need a language to speak about ecology, but if it is not tied to stories that cultivate an intense and honest appreciation for nature, then all the well intentioned environmental education in the world is nothing more than one more set of facts for a child to memorize to pass a test to get through school. More than anything else, environmental education should be a key that unlocks the art of learning to love and see nature as it really is.

People can and do develop a fondness for nature on their own. Early positive experiences in nature — followed by later, more profound, almost mystical encounters with land and animals — lead to an ecological conscience rooted in love for the land. There is no substitute for inspirational people who already do love nature. A shocking number of teachers have never been camping, let alone gotten their hands dirty or bloody harvesting food they eat. Why we do not require anyone who proposes to be a teacher to have done all three escapes reason.

A number of hunter organizations including Ducks Unlimited, Safari Club International, The Foundation for North American Wild Sheep, Pheasants Forever, and Quail Unlimited offer in-school environmental education programs and camps for children and teachers.

The Hunter's Moon and the Crystal Ball

. . . and when some of my friends have asked me anxiously about their boys, whether they should let them hunt, I have answered, yes — remembering that it was one of the best parts of my education — make them hunters, though sportsmen only at first, if possible, mighty hunters at last, so that they shall not find game large enough for them in this or any other vegetable wilderness — hunters as well as fishers of men.

HENRY DAVID THOREAU[1]

The sun is waking up! Did we fall asleep and dream? Or, did our stories carry us into the creative ecotone of the mind where dreaming and waking seem to be the same numinous now?

The storm has flown away and all that remains of the fire are a few glowing coals. Before setting out, let us stir up the fire one last time, brew up a fresh pot of coffee, and contemplate the future of hunting.

Hunting in the 21st century and beyond. What will it be like? Will there be any at all? The answers must come back as questions. For whom? Where? How? When? For how much money?

The hunting instinct will not vanish from our psyche, even if no hunting is done for centuries. Instincts are genetically transmitted templates of consciousness, arising from the deep pools of the soul. They take shape as symbols in our dreams because we are made from nature. Even if bears and big cats die off, which seems highly unlikely in the near future, they will live inside of us. People dream of Paleolithic species, even if they have been extinct for thousands of years. What Freud and others have taught us is that while instincts can be pushed back down into the unconscious, they can and do sneak out in various ways, often causing problems. In an interview with Fess Parker, the actor who, as Daniel Boone, made the coonskin cap an international symbol of a hunter hero, Parker told me that he had often wondered if rising crime among youth trapped in big cities was not in some way tied to young men growing up without the opportunity to learn to hunt as a way to learn to take responsibility for themselves.

The average U.S. citizen eats about 20 animals per year; 5 billion animals are killed for food annually. This does not include imported meat, such as New Zealand deer or Australian kangaroo. Animals will die to feed man. To deny the basic law of the food chain that "flesh eats flesh" is to be like ostriches who bury their heads in the sand. One of the great shortcomings of modern education is its attempt to sanitize, and deny, the harvest of animals, domestic and wild.

Newspapers carry stories such as the World Conservation Union's Species Survival Commission's "Red List" of endangered species, which asserts that 25 percent of all mammals face extinction. The story that doesn't get enough attention is that there is no need to worry about abundance of most game animals. A new problem is overabundance of some species. In an average year in the United States, upwards of 100 people are killed in car-deer collisions, which are believed to number more than half a million a year nationwide. More deer are now killed every year by cars than existed around the turn of the century. In most states, more deer are killed by cars than hunters, and more deer are killed illegally by poachers than legal hunters. Bambi and his family are alive and well! If anything, the problem of too many animals may become as serious as too few, especially when serious illnesses like Lyme Disease, bubonic plague and tuberculosis may be spread by wild animals. Hunting is the most cost effective way to control overpopulations. Already we are seeing urban areas recruiting "master archers" to harvest nuisance whitetail deer. This trend will most likely grow if the general public knows the real truth about hunting.

The 1994 World Watch Institute study *Sold for A Song* warns that 70 percent of the world's bird species are on a decline, and lists hunters as part of the problem. A careful reading of the document reveals that the vast majority of the species are associated with tropical rainforests, and the problematic hunting occurs in areas where there are few

WELCOME HUNTERS SIGN IN WISCONSIN:
In many rural communities, hunting season is a major source of revenue that is critical to the local economy. Will such "welcome" signs continue to be out?

or no wildlife laws. Habitat loss has impacted many species of birds and animals, but in general, in areas where hunting is regulated by wildlife science and law, huntable species are not endangered, and some species are extremely abundant; e.g. the snow goose, Canada goose and wild turkey.

Every culture sets standards for behavior about what is right and wrong, including sanctioning what can be killed — when, how and by whom. Cultural norms vary from place to place. The future of hunting in the modern world hangs on its perceived significance, as well as ownership of the land and animals. Some states, provinces and countries have passed laws and constitutional amendments to ensure that future generations will be able to hunt and fish. While this helps, anything that can be voted in can also be voted out.

Access to huntable lands is often the most difficult problem for modern hunters. As acreage grows smaller near urban areas, regulations increase on public lands. Seeking a dream hunt, the hunter travels farther and pays more and more. On private lands everywhere, costs escalate. Increasingly, hunters

turn to game farms to hunt free-ranging animals that have been raised to be hunted. The conditions may, or may not, approximate hunting wild animals, but surely this is a much more honest way to put meat on the table than assuming that it magically appears at the supermarket, wrapped in cellophane, originating from a replicator like on a Star Trek spaceship. Hunting of some form will endure, but the crystal ball is cloudy.

At a time when many hunters feel driven to retreat into secrecy because of criticism, no ethical hunter can afford not to stand up for what he believes, especially if hunting is to be passed along to future generations. Hunters do a good job talking to themselves, but non-hunters must understand hunting if it is to survive much longer. Never forget, hunters are a minority group. Hunters need to continue and expand their record of service, but the future of hunting may well hang more on telling a good hunting story than ever before in human history.

Conserving the Image of Hunting
In the 1970s, Dr. Steven Kellert at Yale University conducted a national survey of

hunters, which among other things, asked people why they hunt. What came back was that about 45.5 percent said they hunted for meat to put on the table. Another 38.5 percent said they hunted as a sport or a hobby. A third category, 17 percent who Dr. Kellert termed nature hunters, said they hunted because of a deep "affection, respect and reverence for nature."[2]

For rural people, especially those who are retired or on low-incomes, hunting may be an important source of protein, perhaps essential. However, as we move into the 21st century and people are more conscious of what they eat, a variety of low-fat, low-cholesterol, and high protein red meats — venison, buffalo, kangaroo, ostrich — are available at nearby grocery stores for prices that are not much more expensive than quality beef or pork. In survey research, language and cultural norms often influence the responses you get. Kellert's results could be skewed if putting the feel of hunting into words is difficult. People in the 1970s were reluctant to speak about spirituality that did not easily fit into well-defined religious concepts. One might suspect that the percentage of nature hunters is actually much higher, especially among those who have hunted for several years.

Even if we do not hunt for food, there remains an important need for many to hunt to inspire the soul. For many people, hunting is a recreational ritual. Dr. Randall Eaton, author

and videographer, suggests we might call a spade a spade, and change the language of hunting to more closely describe what really is going on.

I recommend that we call it recreational hunting (as opposed to "sport" hunting) precisely because the word means re-creational. Re-creational hunting is a ritual that establishes a relationship of mutual interdependence with animals and nature. Hunting is a ritual that honors the animals and the Earth on which the hunter depends spiritually and physically. We cannot live without hunting, and the animals and earth will not survive without us.

RANDALL EATON[3]

Hunters Need to Tell Good Stories for Nonhunters

Popular media play an enormous role in shaping the modern image of hunting and hunters. Feature films and television are the storytellers of our age; they make and change the myths that are the foundations of culture. In the 1940s and 1950s, the hunting exploits of people like Fred Bear, Martin and Osa Johnson, and Wally Tabor were prime time television, and celebrities regularly appeared as guests on hunting shows. The Davy Crockett movies — *Davy Crockett, King of the Wild Frontier* (1955) and *Davy Crockett and the River Pirates* (1956) — starred a hunter as a hero and generated an international following. Fess Parker, the actor

---

Our 'hunting instinct' has gone awry in 'civilized' society, where the thrill of the chase and the kill are no longer part of our experience and there are no clear avenues of expression except, perhaps to our peril, in the streets and subways of today's urban jungles.[4]

Kids at Shoot for the Future

who portrayed Daniel Boone in a six-year television series, says that he once worried that
the raccoons of the world would be forced to
extinction to feed the appetite of kids for
coonskin caps. A quick check of most neigh-
borhoods in North America, especially where
garbage cans are stored, will confirm that fear
was unnecessary.

Today, hunting stories on television are
largely shows about tips, technique and travel
geared to the hunter audience, appearing early
on weekend mornings, usually not on the
major network channels. There is nothing
wrong with these programs, but programs with
prohunting themes and stories for the nonhunter are more scarce than white deer. When
hunting does appear on prime time television,
it is usually sensationalized in news shows or
tabloid magazine programs that portray the
worst. When will people realize that the
tabloid media targets our envy of the money
and power of celebrities more than cultivating
a desire to think critically and know the truth?

On the big screen, hunters once were
heroes. African safari movies such as *King
Solomon's Mines* (1937), *Tembo* (1951), and
Snows of Mount Kilimanjaro (1952) portrayed
hunting in a positive fashion and were major
box office successes. In more recent years,
movies with hunting as the major theme have
shown hunters as mentally upset, cruel and
heartless, i.e. *The Deer Hunter* (1978), *The
Naked Prey* (1966), *The Shooting Party* (1984),
Shalako (1968) and *White Hunter, Black Heart*
(1990). This is especially troubling when, during the same time, hunting has become safer
and most all hunted species have increased in
numbers, thanks largely to support from
hunters.

A check of current major video sourcebooks
finds only 14 major feature releases with hunting as a significant theme. Most importantly,
only three major films released in the decade of
the 1990s give us dramatic feature stories about
hunters as heroes. *The Ghost and The Darkness*
(1996) starring Val Kilmer and Michael Dou-

glas and the docu-drama *In The Blood* (1989) by George Butler show African hunters as heroes. The multiple Academy Award-winning *Dances With Wolves* (1990) starring Kevin Costner showcases American Indians hunting buffalo. It is the only relatively recent feature film to explore some of the spiritual roots of hunting. Unfortunately, only the Indians are presented as heroic hunters. All white hunters — except for Costner's character John Dunbar, who is given the Indian name Dances With Wolves — are deplorable, greedy, market hunter-types.

What hunting desperately needs are programs for the small and big screen that convey the honest, awesome spirit of the hunt as it is known by the millions of average hunters worldwide for whom deer, rabbits, grouse and ducks are big game. Robert Redford's multiple Academy Award-winning film *A River Runs Through It* (1992) follows the lives of a family of devout fly fishermen and serves as a model of what hunting needs. For how many people could the memorable line, "In my family there was no clear line between fly fishing and religion," be changed to, "In my family there was no clear line between hunting and religion"?

The only modern movie that comes even close to *A River Runs Through It* for hunting is Akira Kurosawa's *Dersu Uzala*, which won the Best Foreign Language Film Oscar in 1975. This is a stunning photographic gem that tells the story of a Russian soldier's relationship with a native Siberian hunter, where each teaches the other about his world.

Preserving the Heritage

Passing along the heritage of the hunt requires kids who want to learn and adults who want to teach. With the large number of single parent families and growing urbanization of our population, it is no longer a given that kids will grow up being exposed to hunting. Special opportunities to give kids quality, early experiences are as essential as hands-on environmental education. Other programs for adults — such as the immensely popular "Be-

coming an Outdoorswoman" seminars, which
have been expanded to "Becoming an Outdoors
Family" — are equally essential to provide
opportunities for the hunting instinct to be
honored and trained in future generations.

In 1998, when a rash of school shootings
erupted across the United States, the media
were quick to call attention to the fact that
some of the children shooters had been taught
to hunt. One headline screamed "Boys Had
Hunting Weapons," failing to note that most
of the guns were stolen.

The almost overlooked story is that gun-
related crimes associated with schools have
been going down for years. And, an even more
important story that is not being told at all is
that gun ownership among youth may be an
important teacher of maturity. In a U.S. Justice
Department study of gun ownership among
high school boys in Rochester, New York,

Les Fetes De La Saint Hubert

delinquency, crime and drug abuse were tracked in three groups of boys: those who had legal guns (with parental consent), those who had no guns, and those who had illegal guns. As one might expect, boys who had illegal guns were more prone to get into trouble, but those who owned legal guns had the lowest incidence of problems of all three. This study supports the thesis that learning to handle and use a lethal weapon can result in increased self-esteem and maturity.[5]

Public Honoring of the Spirit of the Hunt

Both in the field and among peers, hunters need to strengthen the bonds within their ranks. Hunting clubs, fund-raising events, sportsmen's expositions, field days and special celebrations all contribute to fellowship, which in turn maintains strong ethical standards. But in addition to whatever an individual does for himself and his hunting companions, each modern hunter also has an obligation to be a spokesman, a positive role model, and an ambassador so nonhunters understand and respect the true spirit of hunting, if hunting is to be preserved.

The future of hunting also hinges on translating the spirit of the hunt into ways that are appropriate to each community. There is a natural connection between hunting and religion. In the preceding pages, we have seen how at each step of the hunt, spiritual values hover nearby like wild geese calling. In some communities, that may include bringing hunting back into the church.

We have St. Patrick's Day and St. Valentine's Day, both horribly commercialized. Other holidays like Easter and Christmas contain religious and mundane elements. In Europe, thousands of people turn out to honor St. Hubert, both at the beginning of hunting season, and on his birthday, November 3. Should the observance of Saint Hubert's Day also be made a regular celebration all around the world?

Some may say that it is too limiting to associate hunting with just one religion. Set that issue aside for a moment. Let yourself be inspired by what the people of Quebec have done to integrate hunting into their community with the blessings of the church. When you have finished looking at their festival, consider what celebration of hunting might be appropriate for your community. This entire night's sojourn has been a discourse about the marriage of transcendental and mundane, and that is always a creative matter.

Canada has a long and strong tradition of being a nation of hunters. On September 5, 1971, the people of Cap St. Ignace Quebec, which is near Montreal, began a tradition, Les Fetes De La Saint Hubert. Drawing on the ceremonial forms of celebrations of St. Hubert in Europe, a unique mass was held in a Catholic church. Members of the Quebec Symphony performed a special musical score with hunting horns. Hunters, their arms, and dogs received blessings before an altar decorated with mounted animals and wild plants. All related parties, including mounted police and game wardens, were also invited into the church to participate. The following photos tell the story of the celebration, which grows in size and spirit every year, better than any words. Suffice to say that not only is the hunt consecrated in this celebration, but also the community is drawn together into a bond of trust that affirms certain ethical standards. Blessing of the guns, which serve as an archway for the procession to pass under, becomes a dramatic way in which hunters become heroes, showing their sincerity, high ethical standards, and concern for upholding the highest values of the spirit of the hunt.

Coffee's gone. Sun is up. My stomach is telling me that it's time for breakfast. Time to bid adieu to our hunter's cave. We have passed

The Hunter's Moon and the Crystal Ball

the night in a natural museum. Its spirit has been strong. May it live on for as long as strings of geese pass across the face of the hunter's moon, elk bugle in the fall, and bears seek out the depths of the cave for their winter's hibernation.

Many native peoples believe that they have a second soul, a bush soul, that lives someplace else in the wilderness. Even if we never return to this cave again, if our bush souls can, there is hope not only for hunting, but also for the human race.

Hunters these days ultimately hunt memories as much as meat to put on the table. Memories feed dreams, and hunters must have dreams to keep them motivated. When you lose your dreams, you lose your mind.

JAMES SWAN[6]

Footnotes
and
Photography / Art Credits

Footnotes

Introduction

1. Rene Dubos, *So Human an Animal: How We Are Shaped by Surroundings and Events*. New York, New York: Chas. Scribners Sons, 1968, p. 209.
2. Erich Fromm, *The Anatomy of Human Destructiveness*. New York, New York: Fawcett Crest, 1975, pp.155-160.
3. Melvin Konner, *The Tangled Wing: Biological Constraints on the Human Spirit*. New York, New York: Henry Holt, 1982, p. 203.
4. "Urban Delinquency and Substance Abuse: Initial Findings, Research Summary." U.S. Department of Justice, Office of Justice Programs, Office of Juvenile Justice and Delinquency Prevention. U.S.Government Printing Office, March 1994.
5. Dudley Young, *Origins of the Sacred: The Ecstacies of Love and War*. St. Martins, 1991, p. 129.
6. Ghazi bin Muhammad, *The Sacred Origin and Nature of Sports and Culture*. Louisville, Kentucky: Fons Vitae, 1997, p. 84.
7. Marie-Louise von Franz, *The Feminine in Fairy Tales*. NewYork, New York: Spring Publications, 1972, p. 185.
8. Joseph Campbell, *The Hero With a Thousand Faces*. Princeton, New Jersey: Pinceton University Press, Boligen Series XVII, 2nd edition, 1968.
9. Jose Ortega y Gasset, *Meditations on Hunting*. New York, New York, Chas. Scribners Sons, 1985, p.98.
10. Theodore Roosevelt, *African Game Trails*. New York, New York: Chas. Scribners Sons, 1924.

Chapter 1 — The Hunting Instinct

1. Joseph Campbell, *Historical Atlas of World Mythology, Vol. 1, Way of the Animal Powers, Part 1 or 2: Mythologies of the Great Hunt*. New York: A Van der Marck Editions; San Franciso: Distr. by Harper & Row, 1983, p. 73.
2. Franz Boas, *The Mind of Primitive Man*. New York, New York: MacMillan, Co., 1911, p. 104.
3. Carl Jung, ed., "Approaching the Unconscious," *Man And His Symbols*. New York, New York: Dell, 1973, p. 58.
4. William S. Laughlin, "Hunting: An Integrating Biobehavior System and Its Evolutionary Importance," *Man The Hunter*. Lee and DeVore, ed., Chicago, Illinois: Aldine, 1968, p. 304.
5. Marie-Louise von Franz, *Alchemy: An Introduction to the Symbolism and the Psychology*. Toronto, Canada: Inner City Books, 1980, p. 97.
6. Henry David Thoreau, "Higher Laws," in *Walden*. Mt. Vernon, New York: Peter Pauper Press, p. 187.
7. Robert Ardrey, *The Hunting Hypothesis: A Personal Conclusion Concerning the Evolutionary Nature of Man*. New York, New York: Antheum, 1976.

Chapter 2 — The Quarry

1. Natalie Curtis, *The Indians Book: An Offering by the American Indians of Indian Lore, Musical and Narrative, to Form a Record of the Songs and Legends of Their Race*. New York, New York: Harper and Bros. 1907, p.96.
2. Jose Ortega y Gasset, Op. Cit.
3. Karl W. Luckert, adapted from *The Navajo Hunter Tradition*. Tucson, Arizona: University of Arizona Press, 1973, pp. 21-41. Reprinted with the permission of the University of Arizona Press.

4. Richard Nelson, *Make Prayers to the Raven: A Koyukon View of the Northern Forest.* Chicago, Illinois: University of Chicago Press, 1983, pp. 14-19.

Chapter 3 — Invoking the Gods

1. Tom Clancy, *Rainbow Six.* New York, New York: Putnam, 1998, p.107.
2. Arrien of Nicomedia, *Cynegeticus*, circa 136 AD, p. 121.
3. Joseph Campbell, *The Hero with a Thousand Faces.* Princeton, New Jersey: Princeton University Press, Bolligen Series XVII, 2nd edition, 1968, p.181.
4. E.O. James, *Sacrifice and Sacrament.* New York, New York: Barnes and Noble/Thames and Hudson, 1962, p. 11.
5. Louise Backman, *The Master of The Animal: On Hunting Rites Among the Saami*, Proceeding of the 5th International Abashiri Symposium: Hunting Rituals of Northern Peoples, 1991.
6. Lauri Honko, Senni Timonen and Michael Branch, *The Great Bear: A Thematic Anthology of Oral Poetry in the Finno-Ugrian Languages.* New York, New York: Oxford University Press, 1994, p. 150.
7. Laurens Van der Post, *The Heart of the Hunter.* New York, New York: Morrow and Co., 1961, pp. 39-40.

Chapter 4 — Animal Allies

1. Leonard Lee Rue, III, *The World of the Red Fox.* New York, New York: J.B. Lippincott Co., 1969, p. 133.
2. Charles Schwartz, "Winter Trial," *The Pointing Dog Journal*, Jan/Feb. 1997.
3. Ursula K. Le Guin, *A Wizard of Earthsea.* New York, New York: Bantam Books, 1968, p. 6.
4. Peter Beckford, *Thoughts On Hunting*, quoted from Benjamin Hardaway III, *Never Outfoxed: The Hunting Life of Benjamin Hardaway III.* Columbus, Georgia, 1997, p.41.

Chapter 5 — Magical Skills

1. Carlos Castaneda, *Journey to Ixtalan: The Lessons of Don Juan.* New York, New York: Simon and Schuster, 1972, p.106.
2. Ellsworth Jaeger, *Woodsmoke.* New York, New York: MacMillan Company, 1953, pp. 31-33.

Chapter 6 — Clothing

1. Dudley Young, *Origins of the Sacred: The Ecstacies of Love and War.* New York, New York: St. Martin's Press, 1999, p. 129.
2. Frances Densmore, *Music of the Indians of British Columbia.* DeCapo Press, 1970.

Chapter 7 — Weapons

1. Charles Fergus, *A Rough-Shooting Dog: Reflections from Thick and Uncivil Sorts of Places.* The Lyons Press, 1991.
2. Marie-Louise von Franz, *Individuation In Fairy Tales.* Boston, Massachusetts: Shambala, 1990 (rev. ed.), p.130.
3. D.T. Suzuki, "Foreword" of *Zen in The Art of Archery* by Eugen Herrigel trans. by R.F.C. Hull. New York, New York: McGraw-Hill, 1964.
4. Robert Stack, *Straight Shooting.* New York, New York: MacMillan, 1980, p. 35.

Chapter 8 — The Hunting Grounds

1. Barry Lopez, *Arctic Dreams: Imagination and Desire in a Northern Landscape.* New York, New York: Bantam Books, 1989, pp. 199-200.
2. D.H. Lawrence, *Studies in Classical American Literature.* New York, New York: Thomas Seltzer and Sons, 1923, pp. 8-9.
3. Aldo Leopold, *Op Cit*, p. 231.

Chapter 9 — Codes of Behavior

1. *The New Hunter's Encyclopedia*. Harrisburg, Pennsylvania: Stackpole Books, 1966.
2. Marie-Louise von Franz, *Shadow and Evil In Fairy Tales*. Boston, Massachusetts: Shambala, 1995, 2nd ed., pp. 173-174.
3. Aldo Leopold, *Op Cit*, p.240.
4. Theodore Roosevelt and George Bird Grinnell, eds. *American Big Game Hunting: The Book of the Boone and Crockett Club*. New York, New York: Forest and Stream Publishing Co., 1893, p.338.

Chapter 10 — The Call

1. Esther Harding, *The I and the Not-I: A Study in the Development of Cons*. Princeton, New Jersey: Princeton-Bolligen, 1965, p. 39.
2. Honko, *Op Cit*, p. 148.

Chapter 11 — Pursuit

1. Erich Fromm, *Op Cit*, p. 154.
2. Tom Brown Jr., *Tom Brown's Guide to Nature Observation and Tracking*. New York, New York: Berkeley Books, 1983, p. 11.
3. Jimmy Carter, *An Outdoor Journal: Adventures and Reflections*. New York, New York: Bantam, 1988, pp. 14-15.
4. Frank Speck, *Naskapi: The Savage Hunters of the Labrador Peninsula*. Norman, Oklahoma: University of Oklahoma Press, 1937, p. 76.
5. Eugen Herrigel, *Zen and The Art of Archery*, trans. by R.F. C. Hull. New York, New York: Vintage Books, 1971, pp. 46-47.
6. Marie-Louise von Franz, *Shadow and Evil In Fairy Tales*, p. 191.
7. Jose Ortega y Gasset, *Op Cit*, p. 123.
8. Richard Nelson, "The Gifts" in *On Nature: Nature, Landscape, and Natural History*, ed. Daniel Halpern. San Francisco, California: North Point Press, 1987, pp. 117-131.

Chapter 12 — The Kill

1. Reprinted with permission of Ted Nugent and Ted Nugent United Sportsmen of America.
2. Dudley Young, *Op Cit*, p.139.
3. William Faulkner, *Big Woods*. New York, New York: Random House, 1955, p. 13.
4. Paul Shepard, *The Sacred Paw: The Bear In Nature, Myth and Literature*.(New York, New York: Arkana-Penguin, 1985, p. 179.
5. Elias Lonnrot (Trans. Francis Peabody Magoun Jr.) *The Kalevala: Or Poems of the Kaleva District*. Boston, Massachusetts: Harvard University Press, 1963, p. 308.
6. Jim Postewitz, *Beyond Fair Chase: The Ethic and Tradition of Hunting*. Billings, Montana: Falcon, 1994, p. 68.
7. Jose Ortega y Gasset, *Op Cit*, p. 51.
8. Erich Fromm, *Op Cit*, pp. 131-132.
9. Kahlil Gibran, *The Prophet*. New York, New York: Alfred Knopf, 1971, pp. 24-25.
10. Stephen King, *The Waste Lands*. New York, New York: Signet, 1993, p. 101.

Chapter 13 — Celebrating Success

1. Carleton S. Coon, *The Hunting Peoples*. Boston, Massachusetts: Little-Brown, 1971, p. 119.
2. Gary Snyder, *The Practice of the Wild: Essays*. San Francisco, California: North Point Press, 1990, p. 185.
3. S. Boyd, M.D. Eaton, Marjorie Shostak, M.D. Konner, *The Paleolithic Prescription*. New York, New York: Harper and Row, 1988, p. 75.

Chapter 14 — Service

1. Archibald Rutledge, "Why I Taught My Boys to Be Hunters," from *Hunting and Home in the Southern Heartland: The Best of Archibald Rutledge*, ed. Jim Casada. Columbia, South Carolina: University of South Carolina Press, 1992.

2. Robert Jackson and Robert Norton, reported in *California Hunter Education Manual*, rev. ed., Sacramento, California: State of California, 1987.

3. Theodore Roosevelt, *An Autobiography*. New York, New York: MacMillan, 1914, p. 40.

4. Gifford Pinchot, *Breaking New Ground*. New York, New York: Harcourt, Brace & World, 1947, p. 40.

5. Stephen King, *Wizards and Glass: The Dark Tower IV*. New York, New York: Penguin, Putnam, 1997, p. 93.

Chapter 15 — The Hunter's Moon and the Crystal Ball

1. Henry David Thoreau, *Op Cit*, p.189.

2. Stephen Kellert, "Attitudes and Characteristics of Hunters and Anti-Hunters," (transactions of the *Forty-Third North American Wildlife and Natural Resources Conference*, 1978).

3. Randall Eaton, *The Sacred Hunt: Hunting As A Sacred Path*. Ashland, Oregon: Sacred Press, 1998, p. 205.

4. S. Boyd Eaton, MD, Marjorie Shostak, and Melvin Konner, MD, *The Paleolithic Prescription: A Program of Diet and Exercise and a Design for Living*. New York, New York: Harper & Row, 1988, pp. 1–2.

5. U.S. Justice Department, Office of Juvenile Justice and Delinquency Prevention, "Urban Delinquency and Substance Abuse," July 1993.

6. James A. Swan, *In Defense of Hunting*. San Francisco, California: Harper Collins, 1994.

Photography / Art Credits